A Treasury of Critical Thinking Activities

INTERMEDIATE

Contributors:

Rosalind Curtis
Maiya Edwards
Fay Holbert

Editor-in-Chief
Sharon Coan, M.S. Ed.

Art Director
CJae Froshay

Product Manager
Phil Garcia

Imaging
Alfred Lau

Cover Design
Lesley Palmer

Publishers

Rachelle Cracchiolo, M.S. Ed.

Mary Dupuy Smith, M.S. Ed.

Blake Staff

Edited by Kate Robinson

Original cover and internal illustrations by Greg Anderson-Clift

Original internals designed and typeset by Precision Typesetting Services

This edition published by

Teacher Created Materials, Inc.
6421 Industry Way
Westminster, CA 92683
www.teachercreated.com

©*2001 Teacher Created Materials, Inc.*

Made in U.S.A.

ISBN-0-7439-3618-3

with permission from
Blake Education
Locked Bag 2022
Glebe NSW 2037

The classroom teacher may reproduce copies of materials in this book for classroom use only. The reproduction of any part for an entire school or school system is strictly prohibited. No part of this publication may be transmitted, stored, or recorded in any form without written permission from the publisher.

Contents

Introduction

Today, teachers face many challenges. One of these is teaching critical thinking skills in the classroom. The teaching and management strategies in this book cater to all students and provide built-in opportunities for bright students. These strategies allow students to actively participate in their own learning. Blackline masters and task cards are ready to use and can easily be added to your existing teaching program.

How This Book Is Structured

Management Strategies

This section describes the key management strategies. Each management strategy is given a symbol which appears on the task cards and blackline masters throughout the book. In this section you'll also find helpful generic blackline masters to support these management strategies.

Teaching Strategies

Seven teaching strategies are targeted:

- Bloom's Taxonomy
- Creative Thinking
- Research Skills
- Questioning and Brainstorming Skills
- Renzulli's Enrichment Triad
- Thinking Caps
- Gardner's Multiple Intelligences

Each of these strategies has its own section:

Notes: These provide an overview of the methodology of the teaching strategy and its practical application in the classroom.

Activities: These include a wide range of teaching activities covering the main curriculum areas. They can be undertaken exclusively or in conjunction with activities from the other teaching strategy sections. They could also prompt you to develop your own activities.

Task Cards and Blackline Masters: The activities are supported by a variety of ready-to-use blackline masters and task cards. Suggested management strategies are indicated by symbols in the top right-hand corner.

Management Strategies

by Maiya Edwards

Key Educational Qualities in the Management Strategies for Bright Students

Although the activities in this book are appropriate for all students, they particularly meet the needs of bright students. Linda Silverman, the Director of the Gifted Development Center in Denver, suggests that there are several approaches which work well when dealing with bright students in the classroom.

Find out what they know before you teach them.

This will prevent re-teaching what a student already knows.

Omit drills from their lives.

Bright students often learn and retain a concept the first time it is presented to them. Use drill only for the students who need it.

Pace instruction at the rate of the learner.

As bright students learn quickly, allow them to progress at their own rate.

Use discovery learning techniques.

Inductive learning strategies (such as those explained in the Bloom's Taxonomy model) are welcomed by these students.

Focus on abstract ideas.

Bright students enjoy the challenge of abstract concepts.

Allow them to arrive at answers in their own way.

Bright students enjoy devising their own problem-solving techniques.

Allow students to form their own cooperative learning groups.

Avoid always making the brightest student in the group responsible for the whole group's learning. Allow students to sometimes choose their own groups and work with other bright, motivated students.

Design an individual education plan.

This will cater to different learning rates.

Teach them the art of argument.

Since bright students have a tendency to argue anyway, teach them to understand when it is appropriate to argue and also to understand the reaction of others to their argumentativeness.

Allow students to observe.

Provide bright students with opportunities to observe without demanding immediate answers.

Be flexible in designing programs.

Provide the students with a variety of program alternatives, such as independent study, special classes, mentoring, and enrichment activities.

As many bright students are unable to achieve their full potential in the regular classroom, they can often become frustrated and begin to exhibit disruptive or aggressive behavior. Others withdraw from class activities or deliberately mask their abilities.

Providing activities for the entire class does not mean that the activities need to limit bright students or make them conform. We have devised a range of management strategies for the classroom which allow for the implementation of all the key educational qualities referred to above. Each strategy is practical, flexible, and easy to implement.

As you will see on the next few pages, we have given each strategy an easily recognizable symbol so that when these strategies are applied to the task card and blackline master activities, you will know immediately how to organize your classroom.

Management Strategies for the Mainstream Classroom

A range of classroom management strategies could be employed to promote and encourage the development of the talent of the students in your class. Any of the strategies listed below would help to achieve a positive classroom environment.

Management Strategies Suitable for the Mainstream Classroom

- ▼ Enrichment and Extension Activities
- ➔ Learning/Interest Centers
- ● Contracts
- ❖ Independent Research
- ■ Parent Involvement
- ✖ Peer Tutoring
- ✺ Competitions and Awards
- ◗ Mentoring
- ✶ Team Teaching
- ✦ Withdrawal Program
- ➲ Mixed Ability Grouping
- ✜ Cluster Grouping
- ⇛ Vertical Grouping
- ♣ Field Trips

Below is a sample page from the sections that follow. The symbols relating to the classroom strategies are on the top of each Blackline Master (BLM) or Task Card.

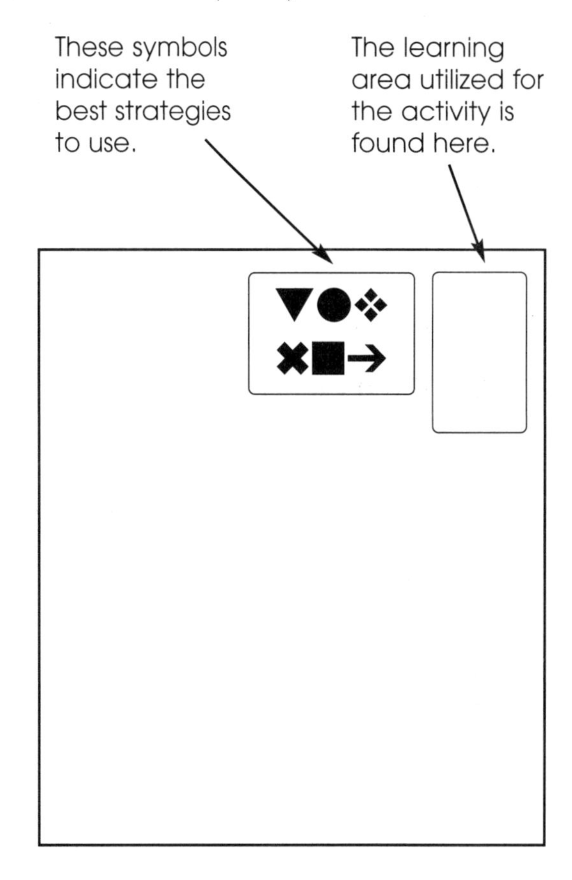

Management Strategies for the Mainstream Classroom

1 ▼ Enrichment and Extension Activities

These can be provided in all subject areas in a variety of ways:

- through task cards or blackline masters for higher level thinking skills
- research tasks
- special "challenge" days
- independent projects
- parent or mentor involvement

See BLM 4

2 ➔ Learning/Interest Centers

These can be established in a corner of the classroom and designed to generate interest in a particular topic. They can

- concentrate on one specific aspect of work being studied, such as weather patterns
- accommodate a special interest such as dinosaurs
- extend certain skills such as advanced language or mathematical skills and thinking skills

See BLMs 4,5,6

3 ● Contracts

Students can be given a range of activities to complete which are set out around the room. Each student is given a list of the activities and asked to mark off each one as it is completed. The flexibility of this contract system appeals to the more capable student.

Contracts also have the advantage of being either teacher initiated or student initiated. The teacher can set defined, targeted tasks or can allow the students to pursue their own interests with some guidance. There is also flexibility in the time allowed for the contracts. A contract can be extended over many weeks or set as a one night task.

See BLMs 1,2,3,4,7

4  Independent Research

Independent research provides an opportunity either within the school day or over a longer period to develop personal competencies through individual experiences. It may also involve interaction with others when designated. The research topic can be teacher initiated or student initiated.

It allows the students to launch in-depth investigations into something that they want to find out more about without constant supervision. It also encourages the students to use self-initiative and to employ their own style of learning to produce results.

The teacher's role changes from being the source of all knowledge to that of a facilitator and consultant.

See BLMs 1,2,3,4,7

5 ■ Parent Involvement

Establishing and maintaining a register of parents' interests, abilities, and availability can be invaluable when planning a program for the brighter students in the classroom. Parents can be used to supervise cluster groups or extension activities and to encourage the exploration of individual interest areas. Some of the ways that parents could be kept abreast of classroom activities are via newsletters, resource packs, and information evenings.

© Teacher Created Materials, Inc.

Management Strategies for the Mainstream Classroom

6 ✖ Peer Tutoring

The more capable students can be paired with underachievers for some activities. This can be mutually beneficial for both students. The brighter students must develop an ability to clearly communicate an understanding of a topic or problem, while the underachiever receives the benefit of one-to-one coaching.

Outside the mainstream classroom, you can pair more able senior students with bright younger students. For example, pairing grade 6 students with grade 1 students works particularly well. The students could be paired for 30 to 60 minutes per week for activities such as writing, computers, art, or thinking games.

7 ✳ Competitions and Awards

Competition and award schemes such as "Young Innovator of the Year" and "Tournament of the Minds" offer enrichment opportunities for all students but particularly the brighter students. Students within the mainstream classroom could be provided with activities to prepare them for these tournaments and competitions.

Intra-class competitions and awards are a dynamic means of extending the entire class. There is a wide range of options:

- 30-minute quiz challenges.
- knock-out quiz challenges throughout the term or year.
- award schemes for independent research tasks. (bronze award for a written and pictorial presentation; silver if something extra is included, such as a model, video, or Web page; and gold if the project is outstanding.)
- individual point scoring for tasks throughout the year. This scheme works well for all students in the mainstream classroom as points can be awarded for both outstanding work, additional work, or for improvement, effort, and positive attitudes, or for helping others. Points can be exchanged for play money at the end of each term, and students can bid at a class auction for donated items such as books, passes, toys, or for privileges such as extra computer time.

8 ◗ Mentoring

These programs link individual students with community members who have expertise in certain areas. Teachers can establish their own database of suitable people or seek the assistance of their district gifted and talented network to provide them with a list of mentors. Mentors can also talk to the class on about specific interest areas and participate in some follow-up activities. This is a very productive way to inspire excellence and encourage independent interests.

9 ✶ Team Teaching

Students with various interests and talents meet with different teachers who specialize in specific subject matters. An excellent way to implement this is for three teachers to nominate three different fields of interest. The students then select which area of interest to pursue. This can be scheduled into the standard teaching week and run for two or three lessons, with a suitable assessment at its conclusion.

10 ✦ Withdrawal Program

Very exceptional students (or "gifted" students) can be withdrawn from a mixed ability class for instruction with other more advanced students. This instruction can be provided by a specially appointed teacher or tutor or a volunteer.

Management Strategies for the Mainstream Classroom

11 ➲ Mixed Ability Grouping

When working on class assignments the students are placed in heterogenous groups (that is, groups with a range of abilities). The more able students assume the leadership roles with the others taking the tasks of writing and reporting. Roles can also be interchangeable, or they can be rotated so that an even amount of work is done for all aspects of a task. An ideal size for mixed ability groupings is three to five students.

See BLM 4

12 ✤ Cluster Grouping

All students can be clustered according to their relative ability in the classroom. Higher ability students can occasionally be clustered for full-time instruction within a mixed ability classroom. This works well when compacting a curriculum for the brighter students so that they are able to progress at their own rate.

See BLM 9

13 ⇛ Vertical Grouping

In classrooms which already contain several grade levels, bright students of different ages can be combined with others who have similar interests, abilities, and aptitudes.

See BLM 4

14 ♣ Field Trips

This involves off-campus excursions to meet with experts in various fields, for example: museum experts, marine biologists, and geologists. Field trips can provide an excellent basis for both cluster ability projects or independent research projects.

Self-Evaluation

It should be remembered that self-evaluation is a very powerful form of evaluation and should be an essential component of every classroom evaluation process.

This has been incorporated into the blackline masters on the following pages.

Blackline Masters

A range of blackline masters has been provided which can be used to assess and encourage students when using the above management strategies.

They are not activities in themselves but are designed to support the various teaching strategies presented in the book.

Teacher Records

For your own records and so that you can show parents that you have given their children the opportunity to express the full range of skills, we have provided an individual record sheet suitable for each student, as well as a class record sheet.

See BLMs 7,8

 © Teacher Created Materials, Inc.

Name:

My Research Contract

Research Title: ____________________

Starting Date: ____________ Completion Date: ____________

Subject Area: ____________________

Brief Description: ____________________

Resources to be used: ____________________

Method of final presentation: ____________________

School time allocated to independent research: ____________

Home time allocated to independent research: ____________

Student's Signature: ____________________

Teacher's Signature: ____________________

Self-Evaluation:

The best thing about my independent research was ____________________

____

____

The thing I found hardest to do was ____________________

____

____

I could improve this by ____________________

____

____

Teacher Comment

MANAGEMENT STRATEGIES

BLM 2

Name:

My Contract

My contract is to ______________________________

I will start on ____________ and finish by ____________

✓ When finished	What I will do	How I feel about my work

Teacher Comment

 © Teacher Created Materials, Inc.

Name:

My Research Checklist

Check (✔) the 3 methods you have used for your independent research and hand in this sheet with your final presentation.

- ☐ Brainstorming
- ☐ Concept Mapping
- ☐ Library Research
- ☐ Interviewing
- ☐ Survey
- ☐ Questionnaire
- ☐ Experiment
- ☐ Graphs/Tables
- ☐ References Cited
- ☐ Have you provided an outline of your project?

Your final method of presentation can be very simple or quite complex. Here are some suggestions. Circle the method you will use.

- Written Report
- Videotape
- Collection
- Letter
- Musical Composition
- Model
- Demonstration
- Scrapbook
- Play/TV Show
- Advertisement
- Comic Strip
- Magazine
- Computer Program
- Panel Discussion
- Invention

- ☐ Final method of presentation chosen
- ☐ Final presentation
- ☐ Own evaluation of the independent study
- ☐ Teacher evaluation of the independent study

Self-Evaluation

Name:

Checklist for Group Work

Other Group Members: ____________________

- ☐ I contributed new ideas. The best idea was ____________________
- ☐ I listened to the ideas of others. The best idea was ____________________
- ☐ I encouraged others in my group. This was by ____________________
- ☐ Something I could improve on is ____________________

____

____

Name:

Questionnaire for Learning Center or Enrichment Activities

Task: ____________________ Time taken: ____________________

How I did the activity and what I thought of it: ____________________

____

____

Future activities I would like included: ____________________

____

____

 © Teacher Created Materials, Inc.

Name:

Learning Center Evaluation Sheet

ACTIVITY	DATE COMPLETED	EVALUATION (for example: too hard, too easy, boring, interesting)

Teacher Comment

Name:

Concept Mapping

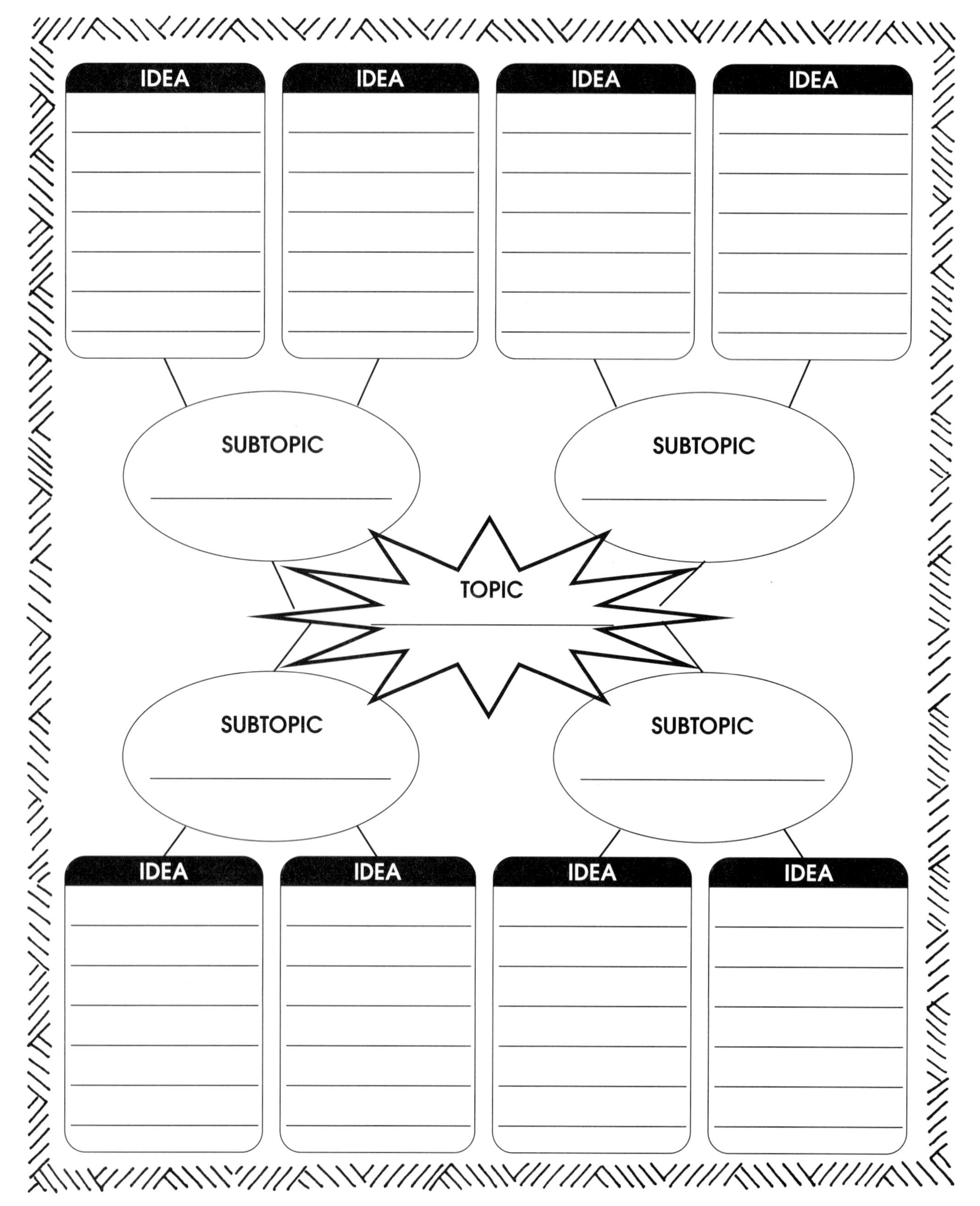

 © Teacher Created Materials, Inc.

Individual Record Sheet

MANAGEMENT STRATEGIES

BLM 7

Extension Procedures

Student Name: ______________________________ Grade: ________________

Students should complete at least one task or BLM from each extension procedure.

EXTENSION PROCEDURE	CARDS/BLMs COMPLETED (Circle when finished)							
Bloom's Taxonomy (BT)	1	2	3	4	5	6	7	8
Creative Thinking (CT)	1	2	3	4	5	6	7	8
Research Skills (RS)	1	2	3	4	5	6	7	8
Questioning/Brainstorming (QB)	1	2	3	4	5	6	7	8
Renzulli's Enrichment Triad (RT)	1	2	3	4	5	6	7	8
Thinking Caps (TC)	1	2	3	4	5	6	7	8
Gardner's Multiple Intelligences (GI)	1	2	3	4	5	6	7	8

Teacher Comment

Class Record Sheet

Extension Procedures

Check that each student has completed at least one card or BLM from each extension procedure.

STUDENT NAME	BT	CT	RS	QB	RT	TC	GI	COMMENT

 © Teacher Created Materials, Inc.

Register of Parents' Interests

PARENT'S NAME	CHILD	CONTACT DETAILS	AVAILABILITY	AREA/S OF INTEREST

Bloom's Taxonomy

Notes and Activities

by Maiya Edwards

Overview for the Classroom Teacher

Bloom's Taxonomy

This model is one of the most frequently used extension procedures, for the development of higher level thinking skills. These skills are applicable to any subject and to any level of education, from pre-school to tertiary. Many varied teaching and learning activities can be developed using this as the basis.

The model enables all students to work through the process of developing a concept, with the more advanced students spending longer at the higher levels than the average student.

The thought processes involved in the different levels:

1. KNOWLEDGE — to recognize, list, name, read, absorb
2. COMPREHENSION — re-state, describe, identify, review, explain
3. APPLICATION — apply, illustrate, connect, develop, use
4. ANALYSIS — interpret, categorize, contrast, compare, classify
5. SYNTHESIS — plan, create, invent, modify, revise
6. EVALUATION — judge, recommend, assess, criticize, justify

Average Student

1. Knowing and recalling specific facts

2. Understanding the meaning from given information

3. Using previously learned information in new situations

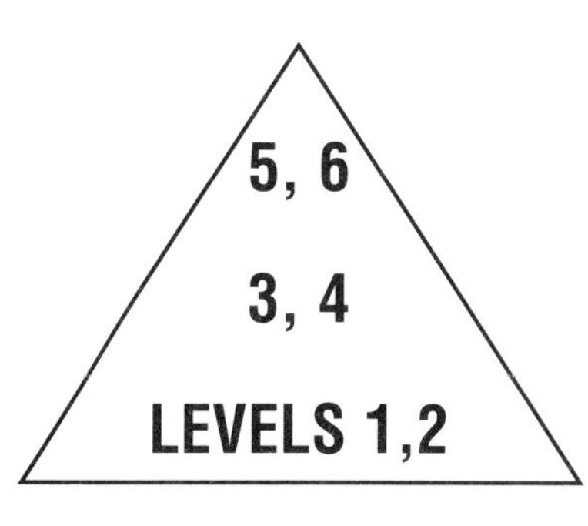

Talented Student

4. Breaking up the whole into parts

5. Putting together the parts to form a new whole

6. Making value judgements

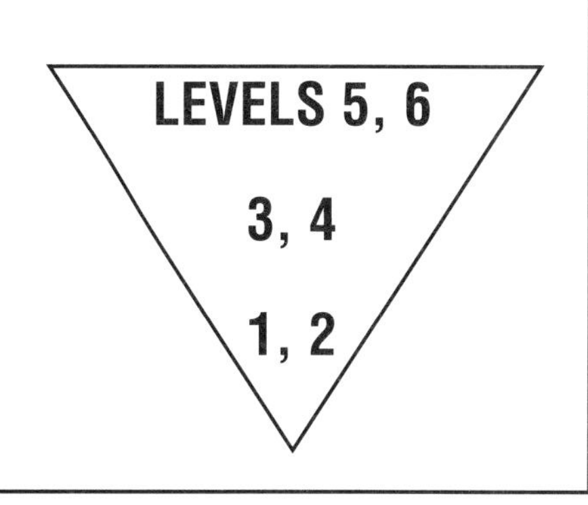

Overview of the Classroom Teacher

From Convergent to Divergent Thinking

Use the actions . . . . to achieve these outcomes.

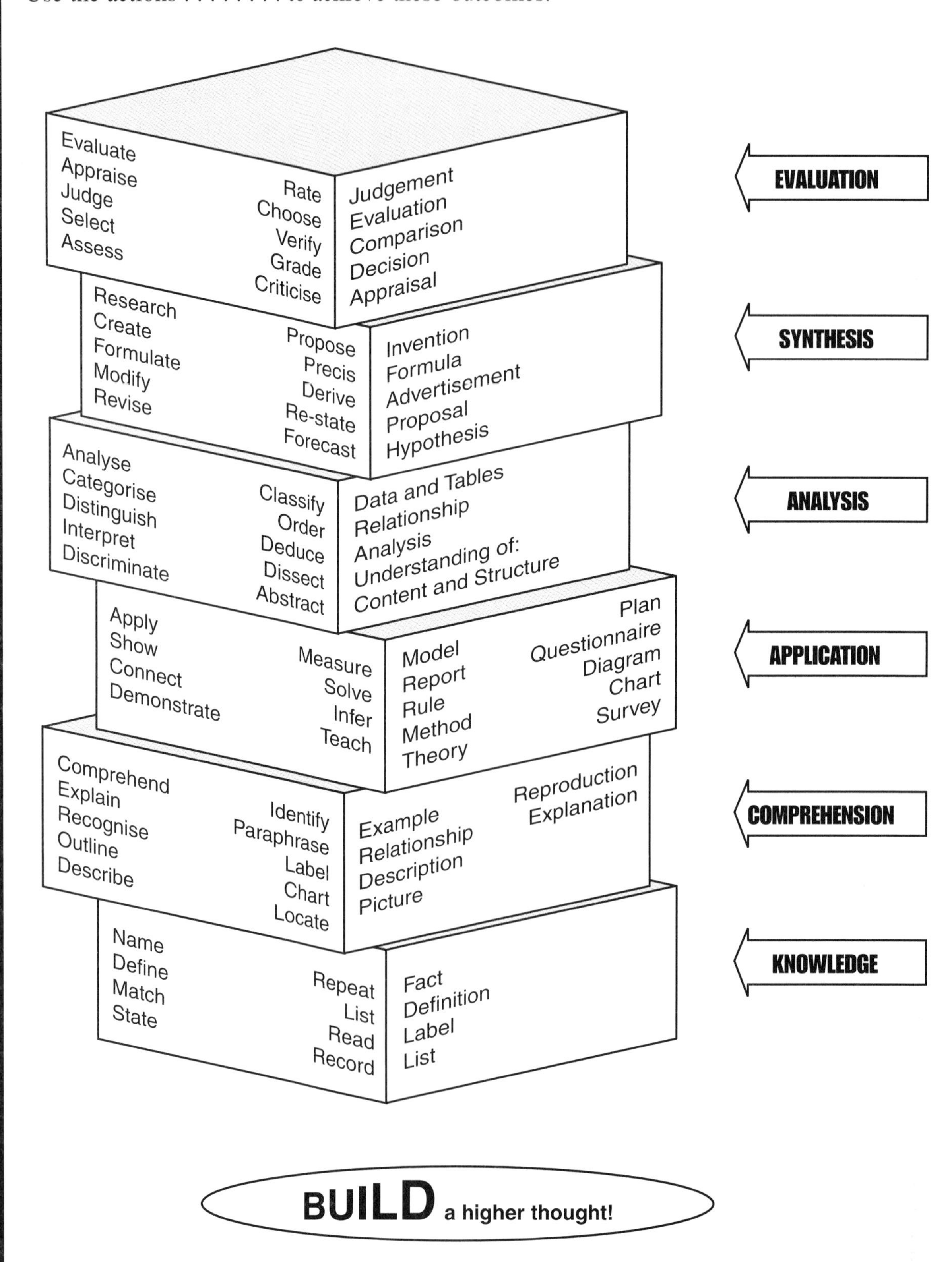

BUILD a higher thought!

 © Teacher Created Materials, Inc.

Bloom's Taxonomy for English

BLOOM'S TAXONOMY
English
ACTIVITIES

Theme: Sea Creatures

Knowledge

- Ask students to brainstorm how many sea creatures they know.
- List a sea creature for every letter of the alphabet. A for angel fish, B for box jellyfish, and so on.
- Present a list of facts that the students have to label true/false, for example, an octopus has nine legs. True or false?

Comprehension

- Challenge students to find out which ones do not belong in lists such as octopus, shark, frog, jellyfish.
- Encourage students to read books about the sea and retell some facts they have learned.

Application

- Have students each give two-minute talks on a sea creature of their choice.
- Make a class collage entitled "Sea Creatures."
- Have students construct mobiles of sea creatures.

Analysis

- Ask students how many similarities and differences they can think of between a seahorse and a farm horse.
- Pose analytical questions such as: "What would be some of the disadvantages of being an oyster?"
- Have students research which animals are good at camouflaging themselves.

Synthesis

- Have students imagine that they have just visited the depths of the ocean with a famous marine biologist and have discovered a new sea creature that has never been seen before. Ask them to draw and describe this sea creature.
- Pose a synthesis question such as, "If a crab could build itself a home, what materials would it use and what would the home look like?"
- Find unusual uses for a snorkel.

Evaluation

- Ask students to name some of the most important ways we can keep our oceans free of pollution.
- Have students work in groups to decide which sea creatures are in greatest danger of extinction and why.
- Ask students to each select one sea creature that they think would make an ideal class pet. Have them present their creatures to the class.

BLOOM'S TAXONOMY
English
BLM 10

Name:

Management Strategies:

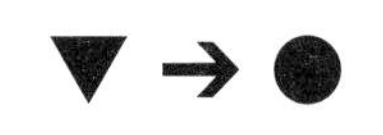

Sea Creatures

Knowledge

What kind of sea creature is this?

____

It has _______________ tentacles.

Is it a fish?

Yes / No _______________

Can it breathe underwater?

Yes / No _______________

Application

On a separate piece of paper, paint a beautiful sea scene with your favorite sea creatures in it.

Comprehension

Tell a true story about you at the beach.

© Teacher Created Materials, Inc.

Name:

Sea Creatures

Evaluation

Make a booklet about the best way to stop pollution of the sea.

Analysis

If you met a shark that could talk, what questions would you ask it?

Synthesis

This treasure chest contains something amazing that has never been seen before on Earth.

What do you imagine it could be?

Bloom's Taxonomy for English

Application, Analysis, Synthesis

▼→●✶

Legend

Write a legend about this picture.

▼→●✶

The First Bicycle

The answer is:

The First Bicycle.

What are five questions?

▼→●✶

Musical Legend

Write a legend that you can set to music.

Design an album cover for it.

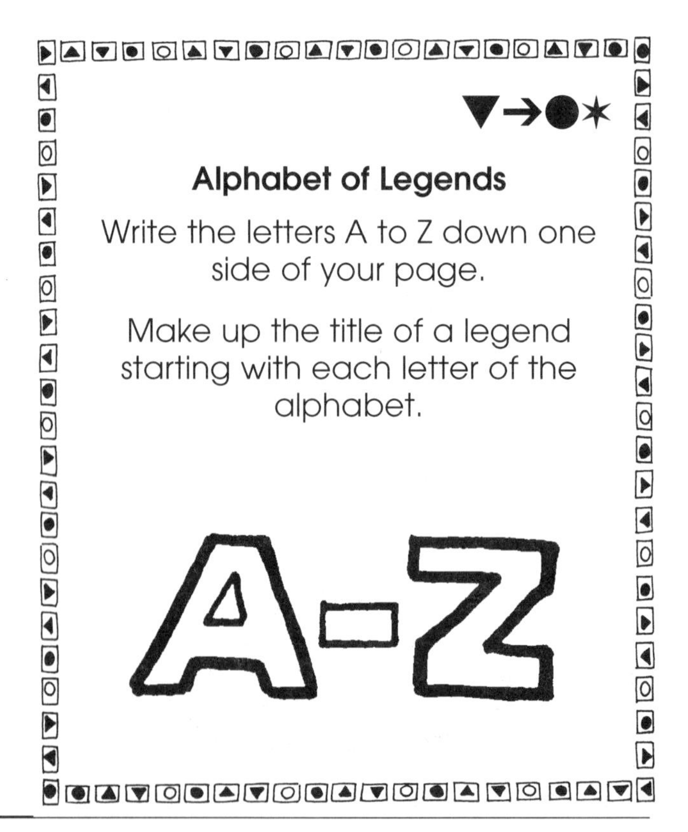

▼→●✶

Alphabet of Legends

Write the letters A to Z down one side of your page.

Make up the title of a legend starting with each letter of the alphabet.

Bloom's Taxonomy for English

Application, Analysis, Synthesis, Evaluation

▼→●✶

Jigsaw Legend

Make a jigsaw puzzle about your own legend.

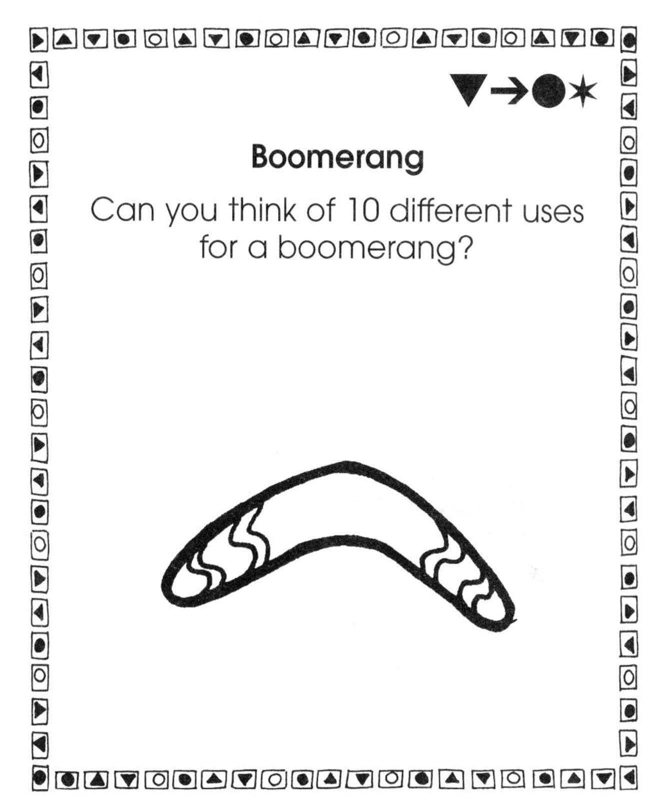

▼→●✶

Boomerang

Can you think of 10 different uses for a boomerang?

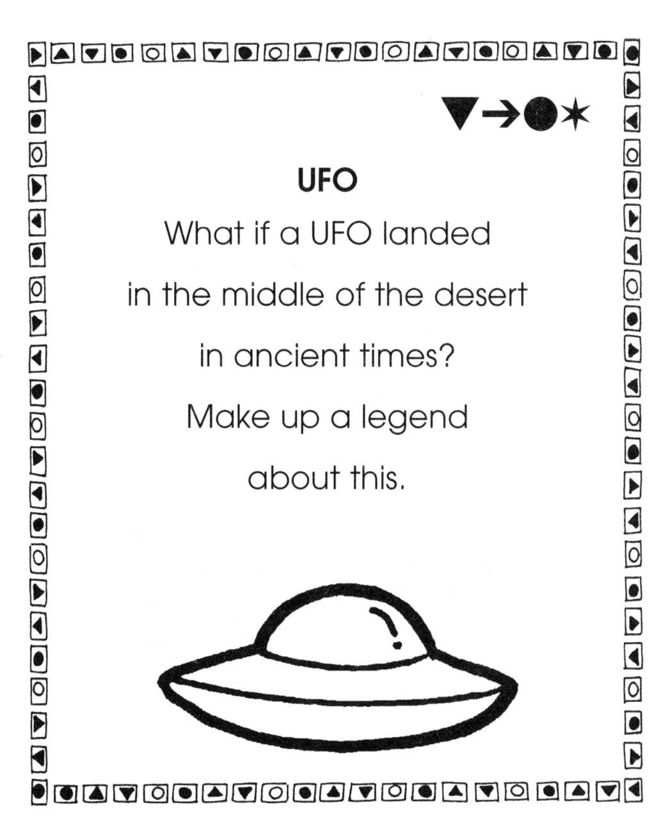

▼→●✶

UFO

What if a UFO landed in the middle of the desert in ancient times? Make up a legend about this.

▼→●✶

Legendary Characters

Think of some interesting things you would like to know about one of the characters in your legend.

Design a questionnaire for that character to answer.

BLOOM'S TAXONOMY
Math
TASK CARDS

Bloom's Taxonomy for Math

Knowledge

- Find out what tables and number facts students know and still need to know. Do this through regular classroom drills and instruction, evaluating students' understanding and providing appropriate follow-up to improve weaker areas. This could include peer tutoring or parent involvement.
- Use concrete materials to teach basic number facts. MAB blocks are very effective for this as students are provided with a hands-on method which helps them understand complete problems.

Comprehension

- Tell students the answer is 50. Ask them what the five questions are? Check students' understanding of the problem by reviewing the questions posed.

Application

- Have students draw a map and write instructions how to find something they have hidden. Remind them to use map coordinates so that they can give clues: An important clue will be hidden at A3.
- Show the students a chart of our solar system and have them place the planets in order from smallest to largest.
- Have students cut out, fold and construct various flat shapes such as squares and triangles, and solids such as cubes and cylinders.

Analysis

- Encourage students to come up with a rough answer (estimate) before doing the actual calculation. For example, before calculating how many words on a page, they should first estimate. Students should also be encouraged to estimate answers to problems such as 49 x 10 by rounding off to the nearest ten.
- Have students find out the favorite color of everyone in the classroom. Ask them to record and chart this information on a graph.
- Ask students to form a line according to their heights from shortest to tallest. Ask them for other ideas to group the class.
- Ask students: to give some similarities between a box and a ball.

Synthesis

- Organize a math evening for parents. Have each student teach a parent a mathematical fact they learned that week.
- Challenge students to make up a number game that the family could play on a long trip in the car.
- Have students work in groups to find five objects in the classroom or playground that are exactly five inches/centimeters long.
- Ask students to find the smallest pyramid shape in the room.

Evaluation

- Have students write out a timetable for their perfect day. Example: 8.00: I wake up and eat ice cream for breakfast.

 © Teacher Created Materials, Inc.

Name:

Math Puzzles

Management Strategies: ▼ → ● ■ ✖ ★ ⊃

BLOOM'S TAXONOMY
Math
BLM 12

1. The two jugs are marked 5 quarts/L and 3 quarts/L.
   Show how they can be used to measure exactly 7 quarts/liters of water.

2. Until last week all the dogs at Bob's Kennels had their own enclosures. Because Bob thought they looked lonely, he decided to knock down 5 walls. That left 3 enclosures, each of which now contains 2 dogs. Which walls did he knock down?

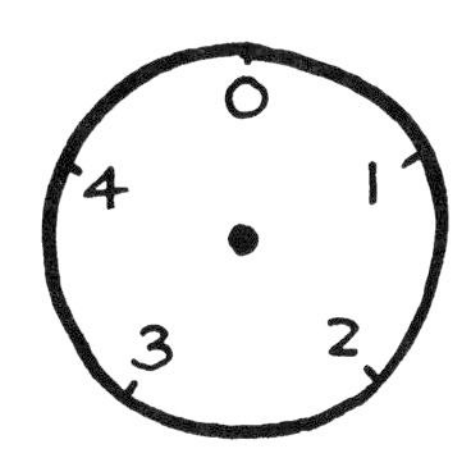

3. A new clock has been invented which looks like this.

- 2 + 2 means start at 2 and move clockwise 2. (2 + 2 = 4)
- 0 – 1 means start at 0 and move counter clockwise 1. (0 – 1 = 4)
- 4 x 2 means start at 0 and make 4 moves of 2 clockwise. (4 x 2 = 3)

What times are represented here?

1 + 2 = ______ 1 x 3 = ______ 3 + 3 = ______

3 x 2 = ______ 4 – 3 = ______ 2 – 3 = ______

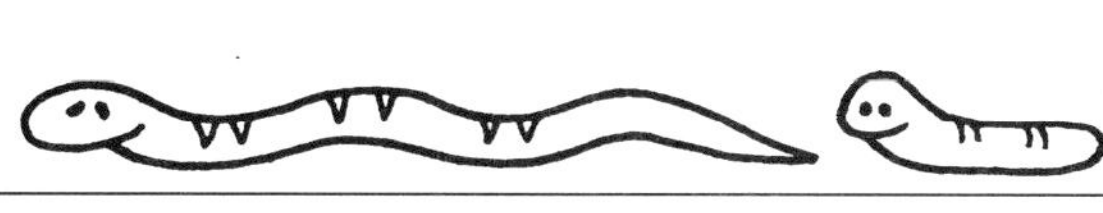

BLOOM'S TAXONOMY

Math

BLM 13

Name:

A New Jail

Management Strategies:

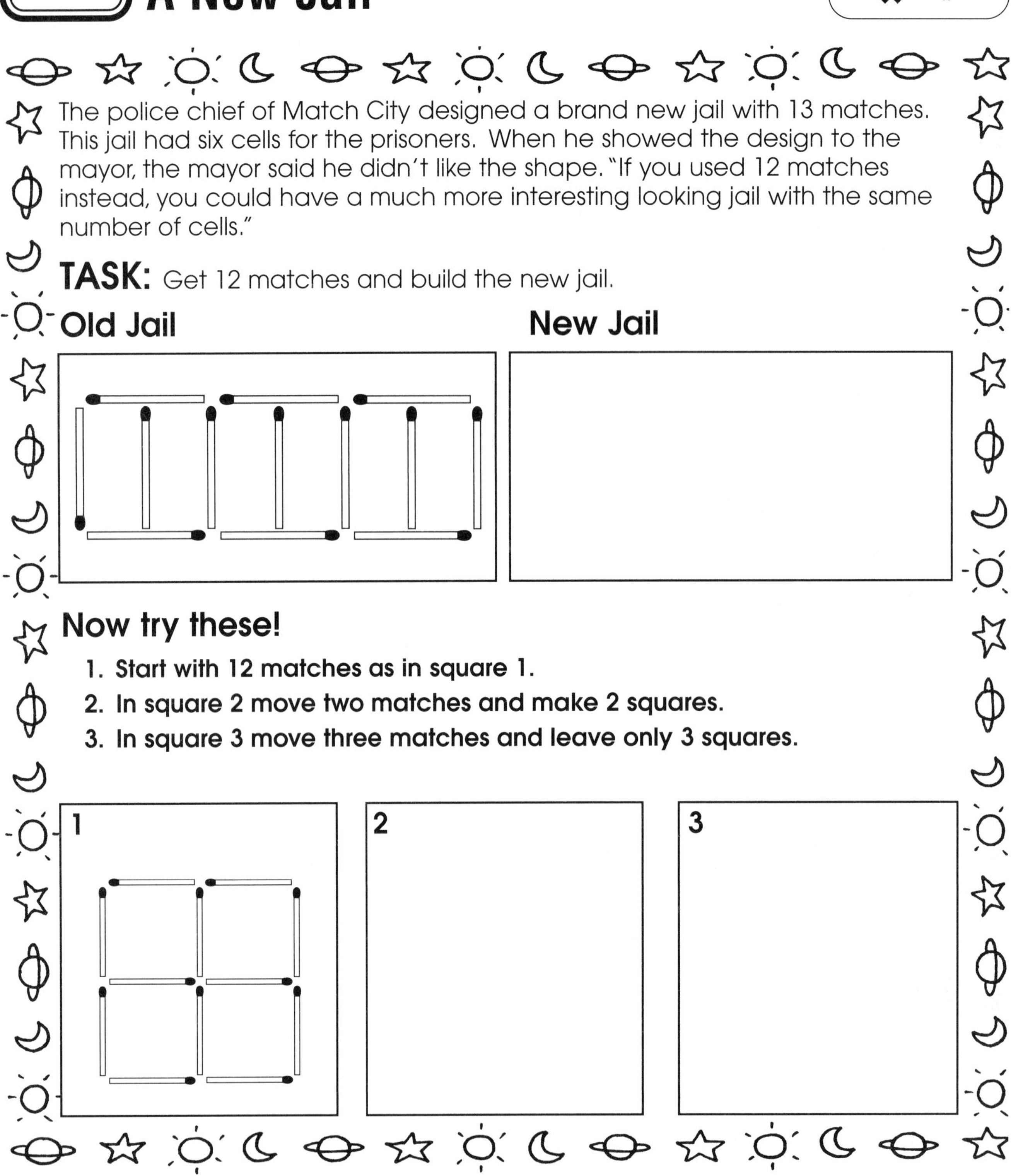

The police chief of Match City designed a brand new jail with 13 matches. This jail had six cells for the prisoners. When he showed the design to the mayor, the mayor said he didn't like the shape. "If you used 12 matches instead, you could have a much more interesting looking jail with the same number of cells."

TASK: Get 12 matches and build the new jail.

Old Jail **New Jail**

Now try these!

1. Start with 12 matches as in square 1.
2. In square 2 move two matches and make 2 squares.
3. In square 3 move three matches and leave only 3 squares.

1 2 3

Teacher Comment

 © Teacher Created Materials, Inc.

Bloom's Taxonomy for Math

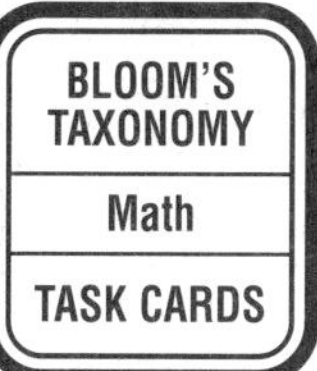

Comprehension, Application, Analysis

▼→●

Make Up a Game

Make up some rules for a game of Xs and Os which guarantee you will always win.

▼→●

Bar Graph

Make a bar graph, showing the number of children in your class who

1. walk to school.
2. ride their bikes.
3. catch a bus.
4. come by car.
5. use other means.

▼→●

Estimation

Estimate and then check.

1.

How many steps will it take to
- walk to the teacher's desk?
- walk around the outside of the room?
- walk home from school?

2.

How long will it take to
- read aloud two 4 to 5 line paragraphs?
- fill a mug of water using an egg cup?
- hop on one leg twenty times?

Bloom's Taxonomy for Math

Analysis, Synthesis, Evaluation

Measurement

Devise a new form of measurement.

Use it to measure
- your book.
- your friend.
- the width of your classroom.

Birthday Cake

Cut the birthday cake into 8 pieces with only 3 cuts.

Time

All the clocks have stopped.

How many different ways can you invent to measure time?

Which one do you think would work best?

Why?

 © Teacher Created Materials, Inc.

Bloom's Taxonomy for Science

Theme: Growing Plants

Knowledge

- Establish what students already know about growing plants.
- List the plants that grow from seeds, bulbs, and cuttings. Put up wall charts around the room headed: "These things grow from seeds," "These plants grow from bulbs," "These plants grow from cuttings."
- Ask students to bring in seed packets and read the instructions on the backs of the packets. Discuss the way that the instructions are structured. Write them on the board.
- Give examples of fast-growing plants such as beans. Ask students if they know any others.

Comprehension

- Copy and enlarge the information contained on the packets. Have students work in groups. Ask each student to choose a seed packet and explain the planting instructions to the group.
- Use the planting instructions and growing procedures as a basis for a close exercise for the class.
- Have students work in pairs. Give each pair jumbled planting instructions. Have students cut up and re-order the text so that it makes sense.

Application

- Plant seeds, bulbs, and cuttings.
- Have students classify the plants.
- Ask each student to prepare talks on the planting of bulbs.

Analysis

- Have students write their own step-by-step instructions for how to plant and care for a seed or a bulb. Some of the stages in the instructions should include preparation of the soil, planting of seed, watering the plant and picking the ripe fruit or vegetable.
- Plot graphs to record growth. This can be done daily or weekly according to how fast the plant grows.
- Ask students to show the life cycles of different plants. A flower could be shown as a seed, a bud, a full-blown bloom, and then as dry and wilting.

Synthesis

- Discuss with students the theory that music may help plants grow. Ask them why they think this may be so and whether they believe it is true. Challenge students to compose appropriate songs to sing to their plants to help them grow. Remind them it would have to be peaceful and soothing so that the plants could respond. Brainstorm tunes, which could be appropriate. Have students discuss their results in groups of 4 to 5 and select a group representative to state their group's opinion.

Evaluation

- Ask students to compile a report on their project about growing things. They could report on planting and caring procedures, as well as the success of their project, and give recommendations for future planting.

BLOOM'S TAXONOMY
Science
BLM 14

Name:

Planting

Management Strategies:

Analysis and Synthesis

TASK 1: In the left-hand side of the table below, write your own directions for planting something. On the right-hand side, draw a picture for each step to help make your instructions clearer.

Instructions for planting: ______________________	
Preparation of soil:	
Directions for planting:	
Watering instructions:	

TASK 2: Exchange your planting instructions with a friend.

How easy to follow are the instructions and how can they be improved?

Friend's Comment	Teacher Comment

 © Teacher Created Materials, Inc.

Bloom's Taxonomy in Physical Education

BLOOM'S TAXONOMY
Physical Education
ACTIVITIES

Theme: Basketball Game

Knowledge

- Ask students if they have ever watched or played basketball.
- Find out if they know how many players there are on each team.
- Check their understanding of the aim of the game.

Comprehension

- Have students describe a game of basketball.
- Draw a diagram of the basketball court.

Application

- Have students work in groups to cut out sports articles from the newspaper. Ask them to discuss and then list the main features of the articles. Have students imagine they are sports reporters who have been asked to write an article on a basketball game.
- Ask students to draw or make a model of a basketball court.
- Have students demonstrate how to dribble the basketball.

Analysis

- Discuss the rules of a basketball game. Ask students why they are necessary.
- Analyze the skills required to play basketball.
- Ask students to compare and contrast a game of volleyball with a game of basketball.

Synthesis

- Have students rewrite the rules to suit a basketball game played on ice.
- Suggest that students make up a five-minute group play based around a basketball game.
- Research the lives of well-known basketball stars.

Evaluation

- Ask students to work in groups to examine the rules of the basketball game and decide if any need to be changed.
- Discuss the reasons that basketball is so popular.
- Ask students whether they think basketball is a good game to play in order to improve fitness.
- Ask them to rate the best professional basketball players from one to ten and justify their answers.

BLOOM'S TAXONOMY
Physical Education
BLM 15

Name:

A New Game

Management Strategies:

Analysis and Synthesis

TASK: Prepare a storyboard to advertise the new basketball game you have invented. Use the boxes to draw your cartoons and put any dialogue, directions, special effects, or music in the lines below. These boxes will be used to develop the script for the promotional commercial of your new game.

I have called my new version of basketball ______________________

1

2

3

1

2

3

Teacher Comment

Bloom's Taxonomy in Social Studies

BLOOM'S TAXONOMY
Social Studies
ACTIVITIES

Theme: Changes in Our Environment

Knowledge

- Establish what students understand by the word "environment." Students could brainstorm their ideas and then the word could be checked in the dictionary.
- List the changes students have noticed in their local environment, for example, more buildings, fewer native animals.

Comprehension

- Locate some of the main areas of change in the school environment.
- Ask students to explain why some of the changes may be occurring.

Application

- Ask students to demonstrate how one of the changes affects their lives. They could do this in the form of a model, a flow chart, or an illustration.
- Have students graph some of the changes in their local environment. Bar graphs, pie graphs, or picture graphs could be used to show whether the incidence of litter is increasing or decreasing in the school playground.
- Have students work in a group to come up with a list of ways that their local community could care for their environment. Examples could be, *use trash cans* and *obey rules in parks.*

Analysis

- Have students investigate the reasons for some of the changes to your local environment, for example, a reduction in the number of native birds.
- Ask them if they think the changes could be reversed. How?
- Ask students to point out some of the regions of their state or country most affected by change.

Synthesis

- Ask students to forecast some of the main changes to our environment which will occur in the next fifty years.
- Have students design an advertisement to promote our national parks. Their focus should be the target audience and the purpose of the advertisement.
- Ask students to put forward proposals to save our rain forests.

Evaluation

- Ask students to choose an environment to study and evaluate which changes are good or bad.
- Ask them to decide on the best ways to improve or eliminate the bad changes.
- Have students recommend four good books or articles dealing with changes in the environment. What is the key message each book conveys?

BLOOM'S TAXONOMY
Social Studies
BLM 16

Name:

The Environment

Analysis, Synthesis, Evaluation

TASK 1: Record the changes in our environment by studying each of the listed areas. The first one is started for you as an example.

Place	Description	Habitat for	Threatened by	If Lost	Can Be Protected By
Beach and Ocean	sand, water, shells	crabs, fish, birds	people leaving their trash lying around	nowhere to swim or sail on the beach	not leaving trash
School-Yard					
Park					
Mountains					
Lake					

 © Teacher Created Materials, Inc.

Make Your Own Task Cards

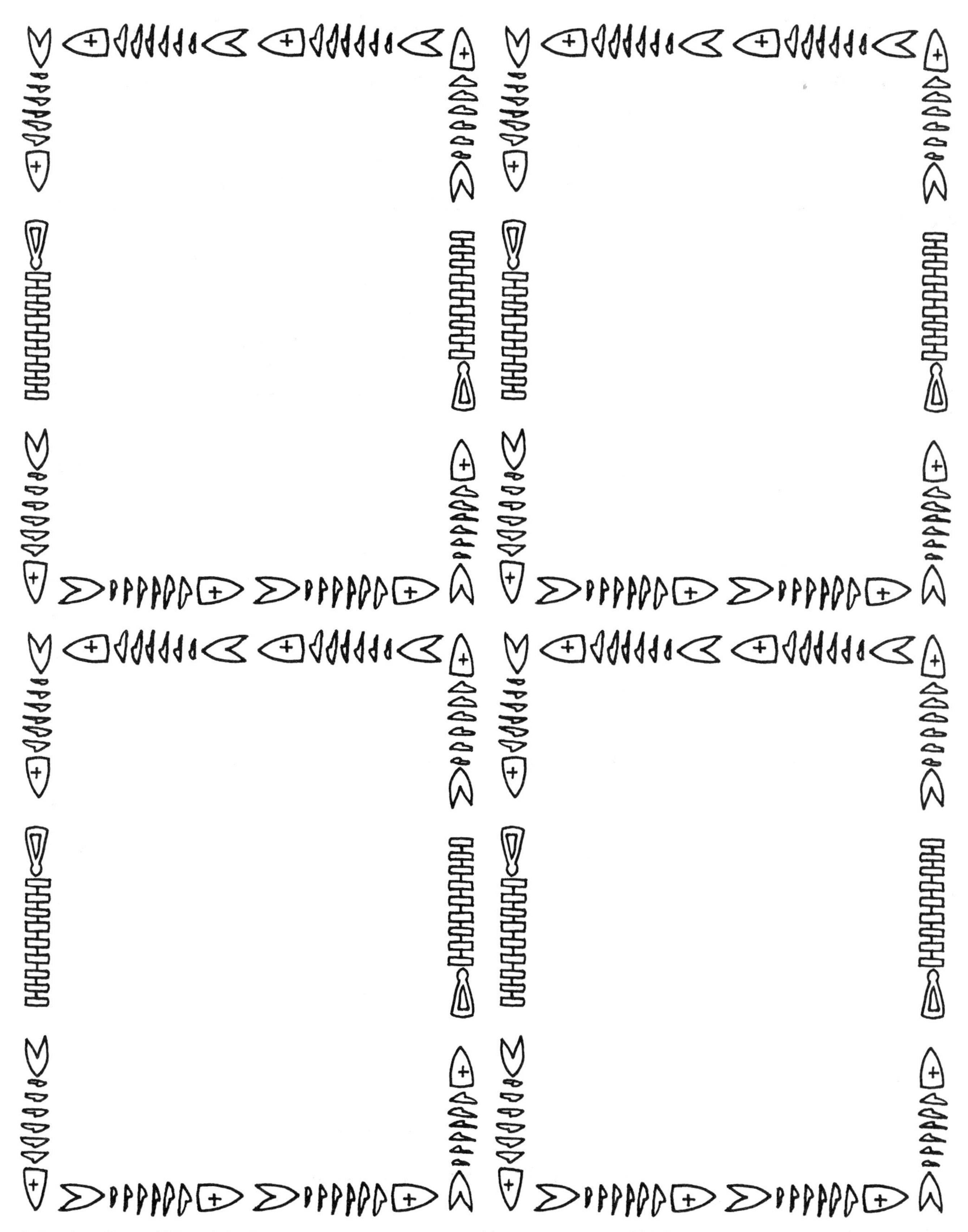

Creative Thinking

Notes and Activities

by Maiya Edwards

Overview of the Classroom Teacher

Creative Thinking Skills

In this section we are trying to move away from verbal and deductive skills and convergent thinking at factual levels to encourage originality, inductive and inferential skills, and divergent thinking.

By recognizing and encouraging the potential of creative thinking in the classroom, the teacher can equip students with the open-ended, divergent thinking skills that are so useful in an ever changing world.

Creativity can be developed in all students. This can be done by encouraging students to become independent thinkers who can modify, adapt to and improve the classroom environment. Teachers should encourage adventure and speculation by creating a positive atmosphere in which there is freedom to reflect, experiment, and take risks.

We can look at the creative process in five stages. Each of these stages involves the thinking skills and feelings which make up creativity.

Problem Awareness

This stage requires the ability to recognize that a problem exists, as well as **sensitivity** and **awareness**.

Problem Definition

The second stage involves stating a problem in a meaningful way so that it is easily understood and therefore requires **imagination, curiosity,** and **originality**.

Incubation of Ideas

The third stage involves the production of intuitive and original possible answers, before the facts have been checked out. Therefore, this synthesizing process of blending the old with the new requires fluency, flexibility, originality, elaboration, risk-taking, and imagination.

Illumination

The fourth stage requires the **awareness** necessary to provide an instant insight into the solution, often referred to as the 'Aha!' moment.

Evaluation

The final stage requires the **perseverance** to evaluate the validity and full impact of the ideas generated.

Encouragement of creativity requires activities to challenge both thinking skills and emotional responses. This can be done by providing a supportive and stimulating classroom environment which will nurture these processes. On the following page are some ways in which the creative elements of thinking and emotional response can be enhanced.

CREATIVE THINKING NOTES

Overview for the Classroom Teacher

Creativity Catalysts

Creativity catalysts can be used to generate innovative and original ideas.

Fluency

This initial stage combines the thinking skill of fluency with the emotional responses of imagination, curiosity, and originality to generate many different ideas, possibilities, and solutions.

Creativity catalysts

- How many ways ...?
- List all the possible uses… .
- Think of all the problems… .
- Give as many ideas as you can… .
- Add to this list… .

Flexibility

This stage combines the thinking skill of flexibility with the emotional response of sensitivity to allow the students to blend the old with the new and to see things from many different points of view.

Creativity Catalysts

- What is the relationship between…?
- If you were…?
- Categorize… .
- Rearrange… .
- Substitute... .

Originality

This stage combines the thinking skill of originality with the emotional responses of risk-taking and imagination. It encourages students to be inventive and use unique and unexpected approaches.

Creativity catalysts

- Create… .
- Design a different way to… .
- How would you…?
- Invent… .
- Predict…

Elaboration

This final stage combines the thinking skill of elaboration with the emotional responses of awareness and perseverance. It encourages students to expand, develop, and add to ideas and materials.

Creativity Catalysts

- Add details to… .
- Plan… .
- Expand… .
- Combine… .
- Decide… .

For more useful classroom catalysts, use the mnemonic **CREATIVITY** to generate further extension activities.

C Combine, integrate, merge, fuse, brew, synthesize, amalgamate

R Reverse, transpose, invert, transfer, exchange, return, contradict

E Enlarge, magnify, expand, multiply, exaggerate, spread, repeat

A Adapt, suit, conform, modify, alter, emulate, copy, reconcile

T Thin out, minimize, streamline, shrink, squeeze, eliminate, understate

I Instead of, substitute, swap, replace, exchange, alternate, supplant

V Viewpoint change, other eyes, other directions, more optimistically, more pessimistically

I In other sequence, rotate, rearrange, by-pass, vary, submerge, reschedule

T To other uses, change, modify, re-work, other values and locations

Y Yes! affirm, agree, endorse, concur, approve, consent, ratify, corroborate

Creative Thinking in English

Theme: Folk and Fairy Tales

Fluency

- Have students list all the fairy tales and nursery rhymes they know.
- Ask students to brainstorm other styles of fantasy writing.
- Ask: 'What might the cow have seen when she jumped over the moon?'
- Have students brainstorm all the possible ways that Little Bo Peep could locate her sheep.
- Have students think of ten other unusual names instead of Rumpelstiltskin.
- Ask: "What are some of the dreams that Sleeping Beauty could have had?"
- Have students brainstorm questions they would like to ask the Magic Mirror.

Flexibility

- Brainstorm the schematic structure common to most fairy tales. For example, do they all contain a type of quest for the main character?
- Ask: "Do you ever feel sympathy for the villains in fairy stories? Which ones? Why?"
- Ask: "What are the main themes of Aboriginal Dreaming Stories? Why?"
- Have students think of ways to prove or disprove the story of the Loch Ness Monster.
- Have students suggest ways to resolve the conflict between Snow White and her stepmother.

Originality

- Have students imagine that the big, bad wolf wants to reform. What advice would they give to help him turn over a new leaf?
- Have students create an amazing place that the Owl and the Pussycat sailed away to.
- Ask students to imagine that they are a modern-day Rip Van Winkle and go to sleep for one hundred years. Have them describe the world they will find when they awaken.
- Have students work with a partner to make up a play about a conversation between different fantasy characters such as Jack from *Jack and the Beanstalk* and *The Little Mermaid.*
- Have students design a publicity campaign to improve the image of witches.

Elaboration

- Have students devise a different ending to *Little Red Riding Hood.*
- Ask students to create a story containing these frightening characters: Cinderella's wicked stepmother, Yeti the Abominable Snowman, and the giant in *Jack and the Beanstalk.*
- Have students describe the character of Robin Hood.
- Ask: "Who is your favorite fictional character? Why?"
- Have the students add an extra adventure to *Alice in Wonderland.*
- Combine the traits of a witch's broomstick and a magic harp to create a new magical device.

CREATIVE THINKING

English

TASK CARDS

Creative Thinking for English

Funny Conversations

Work with a partner to make up a play about a conversation between Pinnochio and Humpty Dumpty or the ugly duckling and Snow White's stepmother or Baby Bear and the Pied Piper of Hamlin.

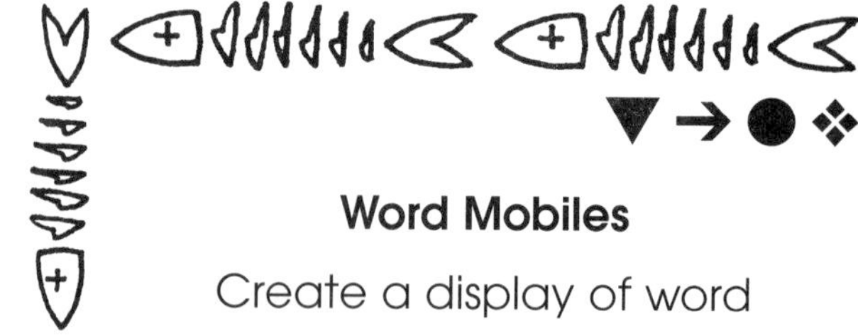

Word Mobiles

Create a display of word mobiles about a fairy tale, nursery rhyme, or legend of your choice. Hint: Make your display relevant to the story. For example, write words to describe the story of *Jack and the Beanstalk* on the leaves of a long beanstalk.

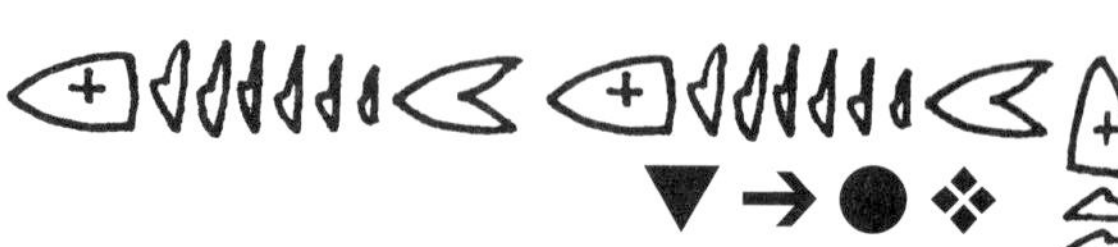

Fantasy Ball Game

Design a ball game based on the theme of your favorite fantasy story.

Magic Castle

Create a model of the ultimate magic castle. Attach labels to describe special magic features.

 © Teacher Created Materials, Inc.

Creative Thinking in English

Pussy in the Well

Work in a group of four or five to plan a trial for Johnny Green for the charge of cruelty to animals. Consider the case for the prosecution and the defense and think of witnesses who could be called. Present your play to the class.

To the Rescue

Imagine you are living in a magical kingdom called Goth. Your best friend has been captured by a fire-eating dragon. Write the story of how you rescue him/her. You can use three of the following:

- a flute
- a pair of rollerblades
- a magnifying glass
- a packet of bubble gum
- a dog
- a baseball bat.

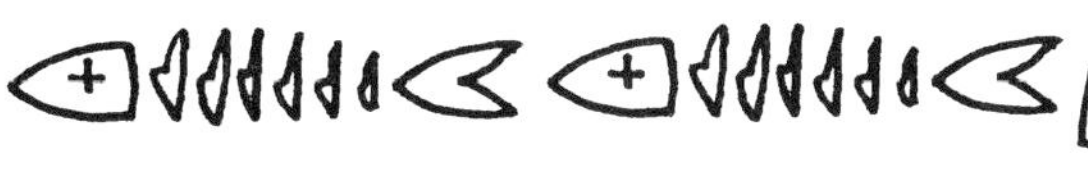

Letter of Complaint

Write a letter from Papa Bear to Goldilocks' mother, complaining about her daughter's behavior and listing the damage she has caused.

Magic Club

You have just been elected president of the new Magic Club. What are your plans for the club in relation to

- the initiation ceremony?
- rules for the club?
- club activities?

Creative Thinking for English

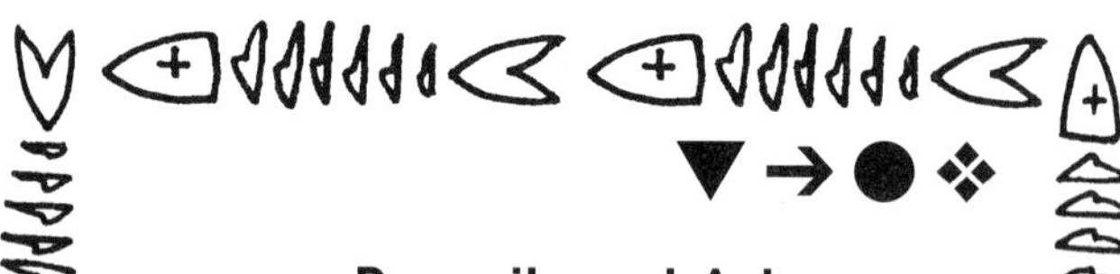

Recruitment Ad

Imagine you are the most famous artist in the mythical kingdom of Tarambala and have been asked by your king to design a recruitment ad. The ad is for brave adventurers who are willing to retrieve the precious Golden Orb which has been stolen by fierce pirates. Design your ad so all the best and bravest people in the kingdom will apply.

Problem to Solve

Respond to these statements:

- You can learn a lot from legends.
- Frankenstein's monster needed a good psychiatrist.
- If the ugly sisters could have had plastic surgery, they would not have been so mean to Cinderella.
- Becoming invisible would solve all my problems.

Magical Product

Invent a brand new magical product and compose an advertising jingle for it.

Accompany your jingle with some interesting actions.

Yikes!

What is happening in this picture?

 © Teacher Created Materials, Inc.

Name:

Management Strategies:

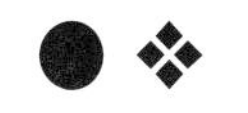

CREATIVE THINKING

English

BLM 17

Magic and Make-believe

Task: Work in a group of 3 or 4 to create a newspaper with a magic and make-believe theme.

Here is a list of ideas that you could include:

- helpful hints for aspiring magicians
- book reviews of fairy stories, legends, myths and other fantasy tales
- jokes, riddles, and puzzles with a magical theme
- interviews with fairy tale and nursery rhyme characters
- advice for make-believe characters with problems, for example, the Beast in *Beauty and the Beast*
- an astrology chart for book characters
- eye-catching advertisements, for example, the latest in glass slippers
- lost and found advertisements, for example a magician's white rabbit
- for sale advertisements advertising items like used witches' broomsticks
- weather forecasts for some of the mythical kingdoms you have read about
- magic spells for witches
- a real estate section featuring homes like Snow White's castle or the Tooth Fairy's toadstool
- an entertainment page full of shows like magicians' acts, balls held at the royal palace, and the Little Mermaid's underwater party

Remember

- Share writing and design tasks fairly.
- Give your paper a catchy title which reflects the magic and make-believe theme.
- Think of interesting headlines for your articles.
- Appoint an editor whose task is to write an editorial.

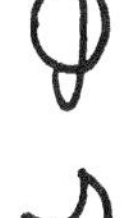

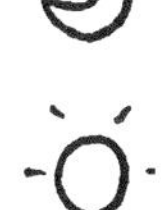

Outline your plan on a separate sheet of paper and show it to your teacher.

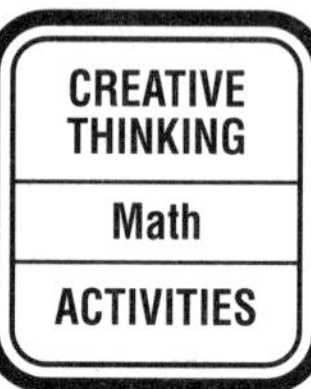

Creative Thinking in Math

Encourage students' creative thinking in math by beginning each lesson with a quick challenge related to the unit of work they are about to study. This will focus the students' thinking and encourage active participation in the lesson right from the start. It will also help to create a more positive attitude towards the learning process.

The examples below show how a math unit can be linked with another subject area, in this case with the theme of television studied in science and technology.

Fluency

Encourage students to think about the thinking skills and inquiry processes required for solving problems. Encourage them to brainstorm ideas and come up with a lot of solutions and possibilities.

Stimulate discussion with questions like these:

- How many people have a television in their home?
- How many have more than one set?
- What rooms are the televisions in?
- What brand is your television?
- How many hours do you watch television?
- What are your favorite programs?

Flexibility

Expand brainstorming activities by adapting and extending them.

Suggestions:

- What is the average amount of television watched by:
  - all students in the room?
  - boys in the room?
  - girls in the room?
  - parents?
  - teachers?
- Which program is most enjoyed by the students? Which is least enjoyed?
- Which size of screen is most commonly owned?

Originality

Encourage originality by asking open-ended questions, providing students with more opportunities to think in the abstract, and rewarding creative and innovative solutions.

Ask students to devise a survey for students, parents, and teachers which will show:

- the number of hours of television watched by each group.
- a rating system to indicate favorite programs.
- a way to calculate the results.

Elaboration

Have students work in groups or individually to reflect upon the previous three processes.

Ask them to look at alternatives, expand on ideas, and add more details with activities such as those suggested below:

- Is there a difference between the favorite shows of:
  - girls and boys?
  - parents and children?
  - teachers and parents?
- This information can be researched, charted on a graph and then presented on the class bulletin board for further discussion.

© Teacher Created Materials, Inc.

Name:	Management Strategies: ▼ →	CREATIVE THINKING / Math / BLM 18

Audition for Trivia Show

You have been asked to audition for a television quiz show called *Number Trivia.* The television producer asks you to solve the following problem:

- Circle ten sets of three numbers that add up to eight.
- You can circle each number only once.
- When circling numbers you may not cross another line.
- You must use all the numbers.

2	0	8	0	1
1	5	4	7	0
3	1	3	5	1
4	1	1	5	2
7	0	0	2	0
1	8	0	7	1

Imagine you have been hired as an assistant television producer. Design a problem similar to this for another contestant to solve.

CREATIVE THINKING
Math
BLM 19

Name:

Number Trivia

Management Strategies:

Imagine you are a contestant in the television quiz show called Number Trivia. How will you score?

1. What numbers are implied by these words?

   a. gross ________________ b. binoculars ________________

   c. octopus ________________ d. unicorn ________________

   e. centipede ________________

2. Which country has these currencies?

   a. baht ________________ b. pound ________________

   c. lira ________________ d. rupee ________________

   e. yen ________________

3. In a garden there are 20 flowers. Seven are roses, 8 are carnations, and 5 are daisies. If the garden had 28 roses, there would be _____ carnations, _____ daisies, and _____ flowers altogether.

4. Five athletes competed in the 100-meter sprint. The athlete from Canada won. The athlete from Mexico was last. The athlete from Australia was ahead of the athlete from South Africa and just behind the athlete from the United States.

   Who was second? ________________________________

5. Here is an example of one way to plant 5 trees in 2 rows so that each row contains 3 trees. Can you think of another way?

© Teacher Created Materials, Inc.

Creative Thinking for Math

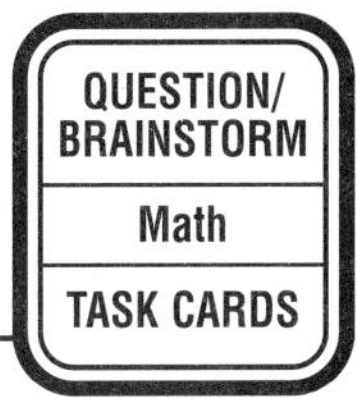

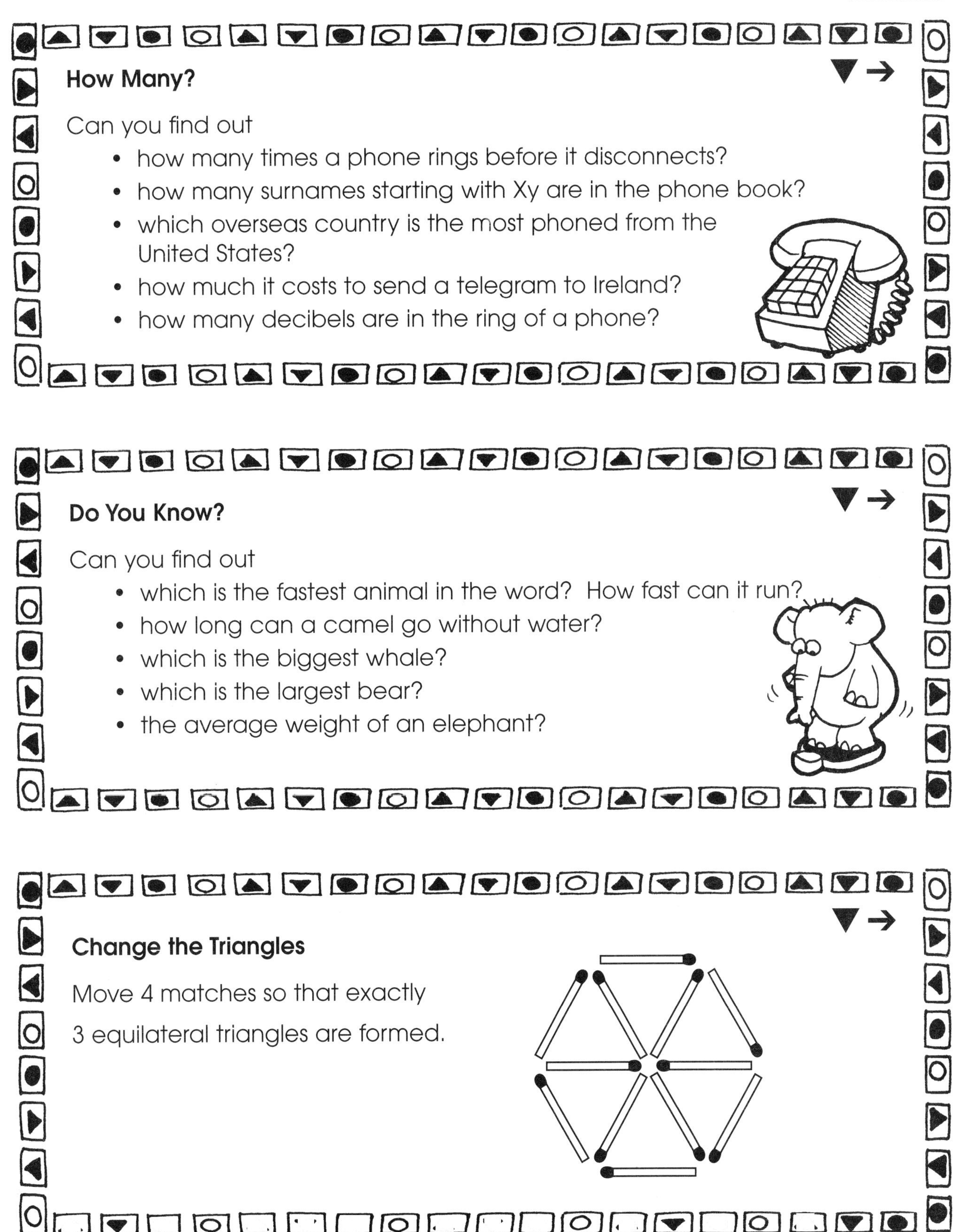

How Many?

Can you find out

- how many times a phone rings before it disconnects?
- how many surnames starting with Xy are in the phone book?
- which overseas country is the most phoned from the United States?
- how much it costs to send a telegram to Ireland?
- how many decibels are in the ring of a phone?

Do You Know?

Can you find out

- which is the fastest animal in the word? How fast can it run?
- how long can a camel go without water?
- which is the biggest whale?
- which is the largest bear?
- the average weight of an elephant?

Change the Triangles

Move 4 matches so that exactly

3 equilateral triangles are formed.

CREATIVE THINKING
Math
TASK CARDS

Creative Thinking for Math

Family Categories

Draw a chart to show all the ways in which your family members can be categorized, for example, by size, weight, gender, or interests.

Can you think of ten different categories?

Rearrange the Numbers

Using number cards, rearrange the numbers below so that six sets of three cards each add up to 17.

12 11 1

10 4

8 17 3

9 2

6 7 5

Find the Pattern

The number sentences in each exercise follow a pattern.

Find the pattern, continue it for two more lines, and then check your answer on a calculator.

91 x 1 = 91	37 x 3 = 121	9 x 9 + 7 = 88
91 x 2 = 182	37 x 33 = 1221	98 x 9 + 6 = 888
91 x 3 = 273	37 x 333 = 12321	987 x 9 + 5 = 8888

Creative Thinking for Science

Theme: Dinosaurs

Fluency

Encourage brainstorming of ideas to stimulate discussion:

- Ask students how many dinosaurs they can name.
- Have students draw, make models, or collect pictures of as many dinosaurs as they can.
- Ask students why they think dinosaurs have such complicated names. Find out their meanings.
- Have students brainstorm how many different ways they can classify dinosaurs, for example, by weight, size, diet.

Flexibility

Expand on brainstorming ideas:

- Ask: "How are the brontosaurus and the tyrannosaurus rex different? How are they similar?"
- Have students classify the list of dinosaurs according to the categories they brainstormed.
- Ask students to design a chart showing the different sizes of dinosaurs.
- Ask: "What sort of model could you design to show the landscape of the dinosaur era?"

Originality

Issue challenges to students with open-ended questions like these:

- What do you think would have happened if dinosaurs had not become extinct? Think of ten different consequences.
- How would you describe life if you wrote from this point of view, "One Day in the Life of a Dinosaur"?
- Invent a machine that can accurately pinpoint dinosaur fossils.
- What sort of pet would a dinosaur make?
- Imagine that you are the last dinosaur left alive on Earth. Explain the reason for this and describe how you would feel.

Elaboration

Draw together the first three processes by having the students reflect on ideas with suggestions such as the following:

- Would you agree with this statement: It's a good thing there are no dinosaurs around today.
- Think of five questions you could ask a dinosaur.
- Find common points between a raptor (a bird of prey like an eagle) and a crocodile.
- Construct a time line showing all the information gathered about dinosaurs.
- Scientists argue about the reasons for the extinction of dinosaurs. What is your version?
- Plan a Dinoquiz. Think of five questions you could ask your classmates about dinosaurs.

CREATIVE THINKING
Science
TASK CARDS

Creative Thinking in Science

Dinosaur Expedition

You are heading an expedition to capture the last living dinosaur in a remote part of the world.

1. Describe it and explain how it managed to survive.
2. Devise a plan to capture it.
3. How would you look after it until experts arrived?

Extinction

The answer is "extinction."

Think of ten questions.

Dinosaur Dilemma

Work out ten different things this picture could represent in regard to dinosaurs.

Consequences

What if dinosaurs had not become extinct? Give ten different consequences.

 © Teacher Created Materials, Inc.

Creative Thinking for Technology

Theme: Television

Fluency

Encourage brainstorming of ideas to stimulate discussion:

- Who invented the first television set?
- Can you describe the first television set?
- List the differences between early television sets and present-day television sets.

Flexibility

Expand on brainstorming ideas:

- What is a patent?
- Why are inventions patented?
- Can you draw a diagram of how a television works?
- Why do you think television became so popular?

Originality

Issue challenges to students with open-ended questions like the following:

- Can you design a television that can be viewed from anywhere in the room?
- All television sets have ceased to work. How many other things could the sets be used for?
- Can you design a television set that you don't have to touch to operate?
- Write your version of how you think television was invented.
- Imagine you have been transported to the year 3000. Draw a model of the television set of that era.

Elaboration

Draw together the first three processes by having students reflect on ideas with suggestions:

- Do you agree that young people watch too much television? Give reasons for your answer.
- Find ten common points between a television and a computer.
- Create a new product by combining the elements of a television set and a dune buggy.
- Write the word "television" on your page. For each letter write an occupation that is associated with the field of television.
- Television was created to improve communication, but in many cases it has been blamed for reducing communication among families. What do you think?
- Rank these methods of communication in their order of importance for the future. Give reasons for your choices.
  - radio
  - television
  - talking
  - writing
  - telephone
  - ESP
  - Internet

Creative Thinking for Technology

John Logie Baird

Who was John Logie Baird, and why is his name associated with television?

Redesigning Television

Draw a diagram showing how a television works.

Now redesign it, using the following steps:

B Make one part bigger.

A Add something extra.

R Replace one part with something different.

Draw a diagram of your new invention.

Disadvantages and Solutions

Work out five disadvantages of television.

Then work out ways to improve each of them.

TV with a Difference

You have been approached by three different clients.

The first client wants a TV that can be viewed from anywhere in the room.

The second wants a TV that can be carried in his pocket.

The third wants a TV that she can watch underwater.

Design three separate TVs that will fulfill each customer's needs.

Explain how they will work.

 © Teacher Created Materials, Inc.

Creative Thinking for Creative Arts

Theme: Fantasy

Fluency

Stimulate brainstorming and discussion by open-ended questions and suggestions:

- How many fantasy characters can you think of who have magical powers? List and draw them.
- Make mobiles of all the nursery rhyme characters you can think of.
- Draw what you know about the seven dwarfs.
- *Little Jack Horner*

  Sat in the corner

  Eating his Christmas pie,

  He put in his thumb and pulled out ...

  Brainstorm a list of things that he could pull out. Draw your favorites.

Flexibility

Expand and adapt brainstorming activities by asking students to do the following:

- Draw three of the things that Jack pulled out of the pie and combine them to make one interesting object.
- Design a magic cube made up of some of the fantasy characters with magical powers.
- Create a different outfit for Little Red Riding Hood.
- Design a business card for the Big Bad Wolf.

Originality

Encourage originality by providing opportunities for the students to think in the abstract and by rewarding innovation and creativity.

Stimulate the students with suggestions:

- Draw the land of the giant at the top of the beanstalk.
- Design an elaborate model which would frighten Miss Muffet's spider away.
- Draw what you think Aladdin saw in the cave after he said: "Open, Sesame!"
- Make a mobile of the scariest witch you can imagine.
- Design a mask for Cinderella's masked ball.

Elaboration

Have students work individually or in groups to reflect upon the previous three processes.

Ask them to look for alternatives or add more detail:

- If the Fairy Godmother had a chance to restock Old Mother Hubbard's shelves, what would she put inside?
- Working in a group of three or four, each group designs treasure to place in the Little Mermaid's treasure chest.
- How could you redesign the house of the Old Woman who lived in a shoe so that she and her children could live underwater?
- Write a description of an original evil character for your partner to draw. For example, it has two heads; one is small and green, and the other is large and red with blue spots. On the green head there is a purple nose with a huge, orange wart, three beady eyes, and a horn.

CREATIVE THINKING

Creative Arts

BLM 20

Name:

Crazy Cartoon

Management Strategies:

Create a cartoon strip which tells the story of all these unusual characters meeting and having an adventure:

- Prince Charming with bad breath,
- Jack and Jill as visitors from outer space,
- Rapunzel who loves to tap dance, and
- Miss Piggy who is in love with the Gingerbread Man.

Design an ending with a twist.

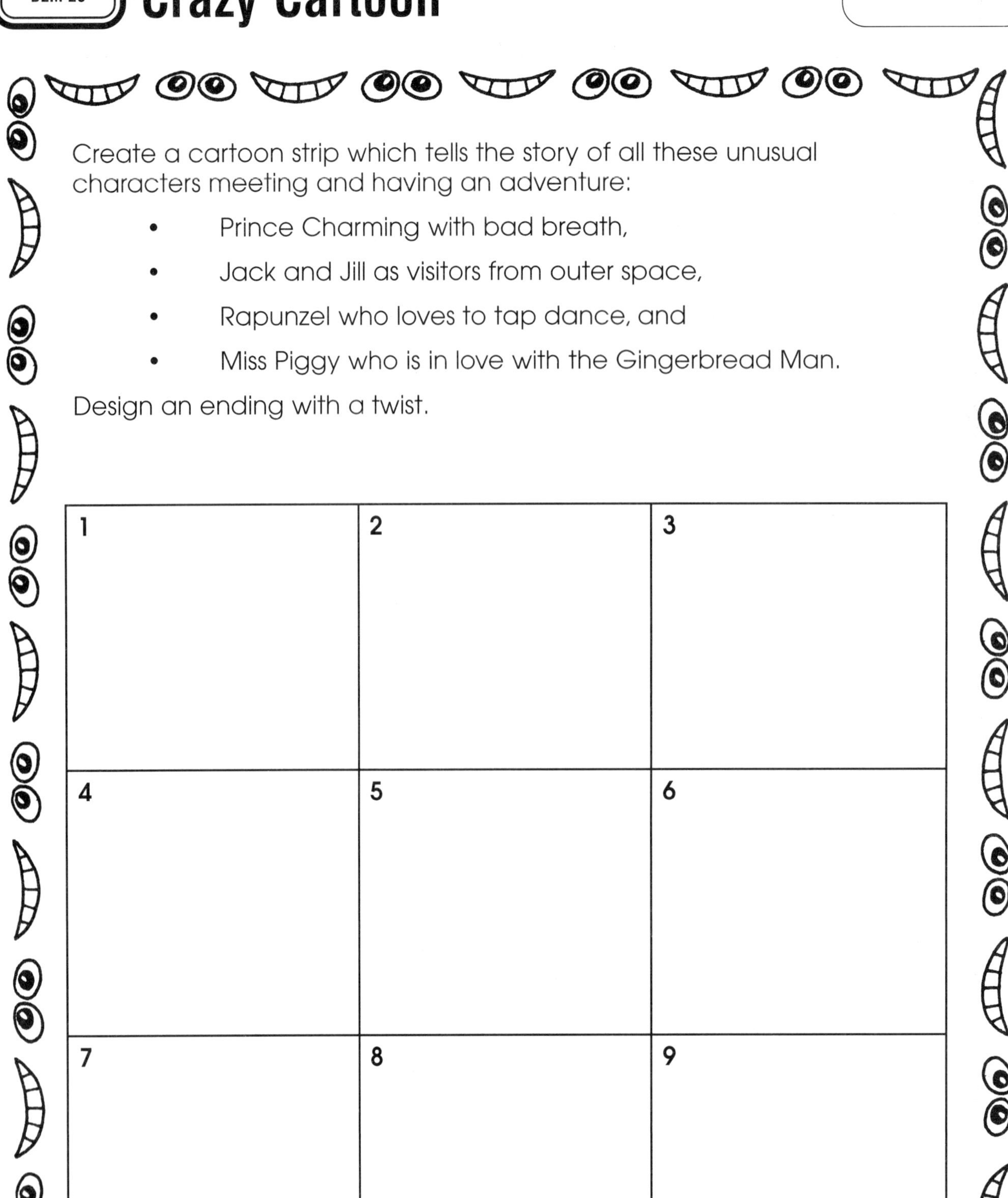

 © Teacher Created Materials, Inc.

Solutions to Number Trivia and Task Cards

(Please note that the questions with open ended responses do not have solutions below.)

Number Trivia, page 50

1. 144, 2, 8, 1, 100
2. Thailand, United Kingdom, Italy, Indonesia, Japan
3. 32 carnations, 20 daisies, 80 flowers altogether
4. United States
5. 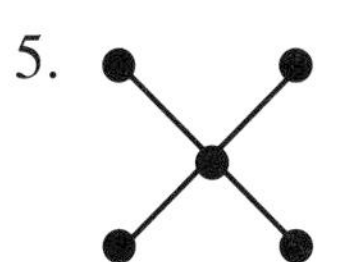

Change the Triangles, page 51

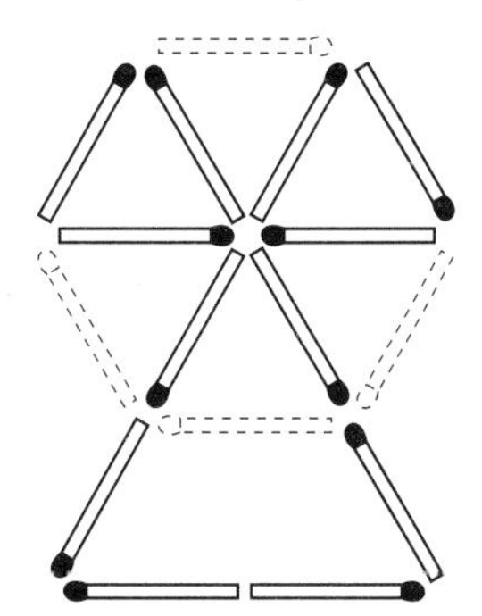

Rearrange the Numbers

		2	12	3		
	6				10	
9			17			4
	7				8	
		1	11	5		

Find the Pattern, page 52

364	123421	988 x 9 + 4
455	1234521	989 x 9 + 3

Research Skills Notes and Activities

by Rosalind Curtis

Overview for the Classroom Teacher

RESEARCH SKILLS

NOTES

Research Skills

Research skills are needed by all students so that they can analyze and interpret information that is presented to them. Information can be presented to students by means of written text, visual input (pictures, videos, computer terminal), aural input (listening to speakers, radio, sounds within the environment), and kinesthetic input (senses of touch, taste, and smell).

Research skills that need to be taught to students:

Questioning techniques help students clarify issues, solve, and make decisions when looking at a topic.

Developing planning frameworks will assist students to access prior knowledge and identify sources of information which will help build further knowledge and understanding.

Gathering strategies helps students collect and store information for later consideration, for example, note-taking, identifying main ideas, and text clarification.

Sorting strategies helps students to prioritize and organize information by using retrieval charts and sequencing information, for example.

Synthesizing skills helps students take the original information and reorganize it in order to develop decisions and solutions.

Evaluation helps the students to determine if the information found is sufficient to support a solution or conclusion.

Reporting skills allow the students to translate findings into persuasive, instructive, and effective products, for example, in the presentation of a project.

These research skills are best taught within the classroom by means of a **research cycle**. This cycle provides students with the steps to plan and conduct meaningful research to complete projects, solve problems, and make informed decisions.

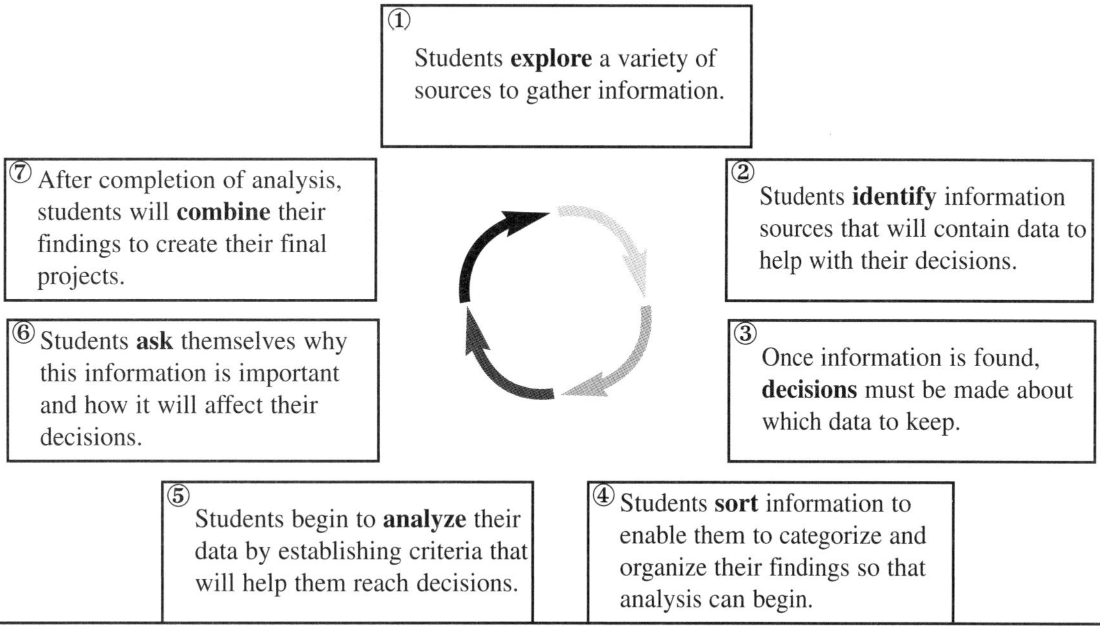

① Students **explore** a variety of sources to gather information.

② Students **identify** information sources that will contain data to help with their decisions.

③ Once information is found, **decisions** must be made about which data to keep.

④ Students **sort** information to enable them to categorize and organize their findings so that analysis can begin.

⑤ Students begin to **analyze** their data by establishing criteria that will help them reach decisions.

⑥ Students **ask** themselves why this information is important and how it will affect their decisions.

⑦ After completion of analysis, students will **combine** their findings to create their final projects.

RESEARCH SKILLS

NOTES

Overview for the Classroom Teacher

The Research Cycle

There are seven steps in the research cycle.

1 **Questioning**
- This step identifies the problem that needs solving.
- Students need to be taught questioning skills which will enable them to identify what data is needed to solve the main problem. It is critical students are encouraged to think laterally and from as many perspectives as possible.
- From the questioning process, students should be able to identify information they already know and formulate questions to locate information they need to find out.

2 **Planning**
- This step begins to develop information- seeking strategies to help locate answers to all the questions asked.
- Students need to be introduced to the range of resources which are available, such as books, videos, people, pictures, and the Internet.
- Students need to plan how to organize the information that will be gathered.

3 **Gathering**
- This step enables students to clarify the information that has been located.
- Students need to develop effective note-taking strategies so that the main idea is identified from the information.
- Students also need to recognize the value of a bibliography so that they can return to an information source if required.

4 **Sorting**
- This step requires students to systematically scan the data for relevant information that will contribute to understanding.
- Students need to classify the gathered information under headings and sub-headings and make generalizations about it.
- The data gathered can then be placed into a sequence of events.

5 **Synthesizing**
- This process is like doing a jigsaw puzzle.
- Students need to arrange and rearrange fragments of information until patterns begin to emerge.
- Students develop their skills so that they are able to answer questions with understanding, accuracy, and detail.

6 **Evaluating**
- When this stage is first reached, early attempts to synthesize information may result in the need for more information to clarify or enhance understanding. If the students find that pieces are missing, they will need to begin the cycle again or ask what more is needed to complete the picture.
- As the cycle begins again, questioning will become more specific and will lead to more planning and more gathering of information.
- When the picture seems to be complete, the students can decide that the cycle should finish.
- It may be necessary to repeat the cycle and gather more information until the students decide that an investigation is complete.

7 **Reporting**
- After the cycle has been completed, it is time to report and share findings. This may take the form of an oral, written, or graphic presentation, a debate, or any other presentation that students may decide upon.

Classroom Design

- Have students work independently or in mixed ability or homogeneous groups, as appropriate for the activity.
- Provide a variety of resources around the room, including hands-on and extension activities and learning centers aimed at different levels.
- Always give criteria for evaluation and a timeline for work to be completed.

 © Teacher Created Materials, Inc.

Research Skills for English

RESEARCH SKILLS
English
ACTIVITIES

Theme: Animals

Questioning

- Have students ask a variety of questions: How many dogs do you have? (factual) Why do dogs have to be kept on a leash when you walk them? (inferential) What are some ways that dogs' leashes could be improved? (creative) Do you think that dog laws are unjust? (critical)
- Have students change statements into questions.
- Provide students with answers and have them develop the questions. For example, "The answer is Antelopes. What are five questions?"
- Have students role-play reporters or police officers. In these roles how would they ask questions of different people?

Planning

- Ensure that students understand the different parts of a book (index, contents, headings, and subheadings).
- Have students identify words they would use to conduct a search on the Internet for information about a specific animal— giraffe, Africa, habitat. Then teach students to further define their search terms (e.g., South Africa).
- Ask students to make a note of relevant pages of books, web sites, people and computer CD-ROMS for their research.

Gathering

- For homework have students visit a Web site about a zoo. There are many famous zoos around the world including the one in San Diego.
- From a print of a Web site (or another resource), have students underline key words within a passage and then use these key words to write a few sentences about the topic.
- Ask students to list important facts they observe or hear while watching a video or listening to a tape.
- Have students underline and check the meanings of unfamiliar words within a written text. Compile a class list of these.

Sorting

- Ask students to organize information according to different criteria, for example, statements about animals or things that are true or false.
- Give students information that has been grouped together using different characteristics, for example, large animals and small animals or carnivores and herbivores. Have students identify those characteristics.

Synthesizing

- Have students debate the issue, "Zoos are essential to our lives."
- Have students role play ways to photograph animals in the wild.
- Have students use given information to help them build models of zoos of the future.

Evaluating

- Have students use the information they have gathered about a topic to answer questions. For example, "How is this animal unique?"
- Have students write a play about an animal being voted the jungle's most important animal.
- Ask students to write a story about a year in the life of an animal of their choice. Have them investigate that animal's habitat and habits.

Reporting

- Have students imagine they are about to interview a ranger from an African game reserve. Ask them to write out questions they would ask this person.
- Have students pair up and role-play the interview.
- Have students prepare an oral or written report on what was learned in the interview.

RESEARCH SKILLS
English
TASK CARDS

Research Skills in English

Evaluation

My Favorite Animal

If you could choose to be one animal which lives in the African jungle, which animal would you choose and why?

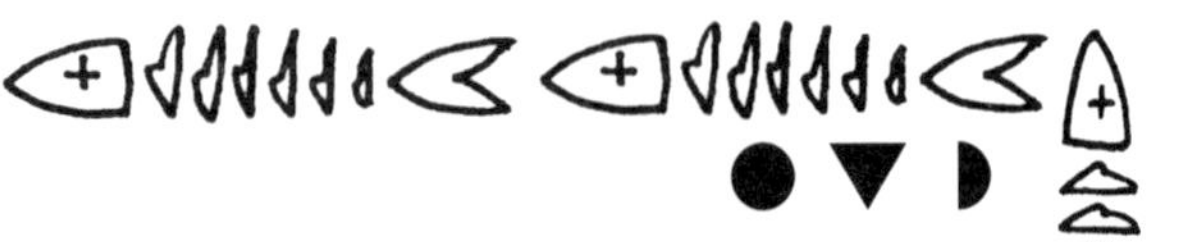

Book Cover

Design a cover for a book about your favorite jungle animal. It could live in the jungles of South America, New Guinea, or Africa. Include a short blurb describing the animal.

Safari

Imagine you have been given the task of organizing an African Safari. Plan your campaign to attract people to join you.

Zoo Enclosure

Make a list of jungle animals that are endangered. Choose one of these animals and design a zoo enclosure for it.

- Make it comfortable.
- Make it very similar to their natural surroundings.
- Make it one which allows the animal to be viewed but not disturbed, by the public.

 © Teacher Created Materials, Inc.

Name:

Management Strategies:

Questions and Answers

Questioning Skills

Match the question with the answer.

1. ____________ 2. ____________ 3. ____________ 4. ____________

2. Which is better, a chocolate ice cream cone or a caramel sundae?

3. Which day of the week do you like best?

Answers:

A. A sundae is better because you can have nuts on top.

B. Turn on the oven, then put all the ingredients in a bowl, mix them, and put them in the oven to bake.

C. Sunday is best because I go out with Mom and Dad.

D. I would be able to buy lots of different things for my family.

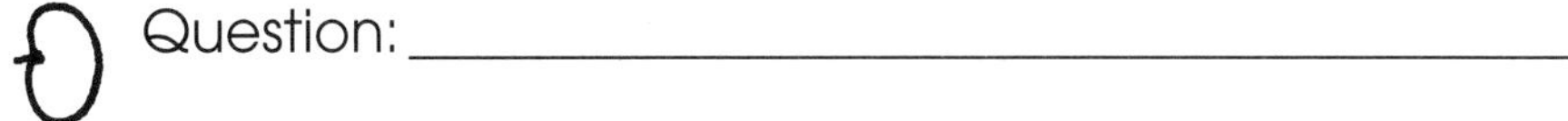

Choose one of the above questions and write down five different answers.

Question: ____

Answers:

1. ____

2. ____

3. ____

4. ____

5. ____

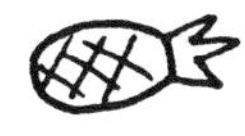

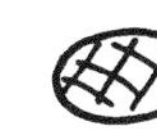

RESEARCH SKILLS
English
BLM 22

Name:

Management Strategies:

Stars and Planets

Gathering, Sorting, Analyzing

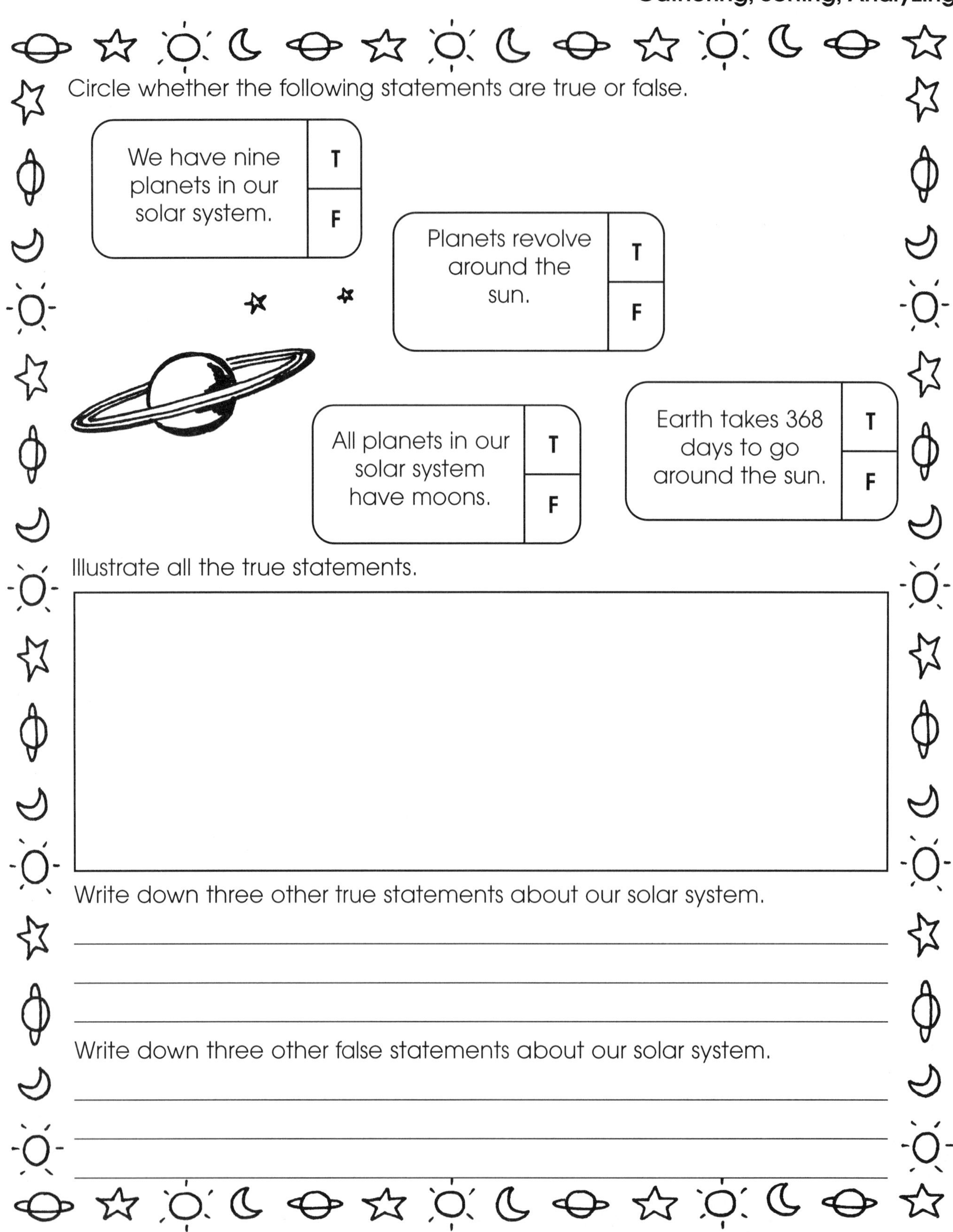

Circle whether the following statements are true or false.

We have nine planets in our solar system.	T / F

Planets revolve around the sun.	T / F

All planets in our solar system have moons.	T / F

Earth takes 368 days to go around the sun.	T / F

Illustrate all the true statements.

Write down three other true statements about our solar system.

___

___

___

Write down three other false statements about our solar system.

___

___

___

 © Teacher Created Materials, Inc.

Name:

Management Strategies: → ⊃

RESEARCH SKILLS

English

BLM 23

Sand

Synthesizing

We find sand at the beach and in rivers. Sand can be coarse or fine. It can be made from particles of shells, rocks , and coral and is often different colors.

We have many uses for sand:

- We use it for building things like sandcastles at the beach.
- We use it as a filling for soft toys and beanbags.
- Mined sand is used to make glass.

1. Can you think of three other uses for sand?

(a)____

(b)____

(c)____

2. Draw a diagram to help you explain how shells, rocks, and coral are made into grains of sand that are found on the beach or in rivers.

3. In the past sand was often used to measure time. Design a new device that uses sand to measure time. Illustrate your invention below and describe how it works.

Research Skills for Math

Theme: Time

Questioning

- Have students devise questions using closed techniques to elicit responses for surveys, for example, "How many hours do you watch television each day? How long does it take you to eat breakfast, have a shower, walk to school?"
- Have students predict how long it will take them to do different activities and then check their estimations.
- Ask students to devise questions that will help them verbalize the process they go through to convert hours to minutes, minutes to seconds, or work out a 24-hour clock.

Planning

- Ask students to formulate a problem related to time and work out how to find an answer to this question, for example, "How was time measured in Roman times?"
- Have students formulate hypotheses about time and the steps they would take to prove their hypotheses.
- Encourage students to have alternate plans and resources available in case one method fails.

Gathering

- Give students information references where facts about time can be located, such as the Web site **www.nsc.gov.au.measspt/timing.html**
- Ask students to locate information about different ways time can be measured, such as clocks, stopwatches, electronic devices.
- Have students compare different instruments for measuring time to find out which is more accurate, for example, egg timer and sundial.

Sorting

- Ask students to sort activities according to how they would be measured, for example, birthdays in years, lessons in hours, boiling eggs in minutes.
- Have students organize information into a chronological time line.

Synthesizing

- Have students apply their knowledge of telling time to reading bus, train or airline timetables.
- Have students devise a timetable for a week's activities at a school camp.
- Ask students to use their knowledge of time to answer true or false to statements such as, "It takes one day to build a house," or "It takes 30 minutes to watch my favorite television show."

Evaluating

- Ask students to determine whether their predictions of time were accurate and provide reasons for their answers.
- Ask students to apply knowledge of measuring time to a new way of measuring time.

Reporting

- Ask students to present their findings about timed activities in a variety of visual ways. For example, if a pair of students were testing an estimation of the time taken to do an activity, they could show pictures of the activity in stages with captions of the actual time and the estimated time below.
- Encourage other class members to make constructive and positive comments about each report.

 © Teacher Created Materials, Inc.

Research Skills for Math

Questioning, Analyzing, and Synthesizing

RESEARCH SKILLS
Math
TASK CARDS

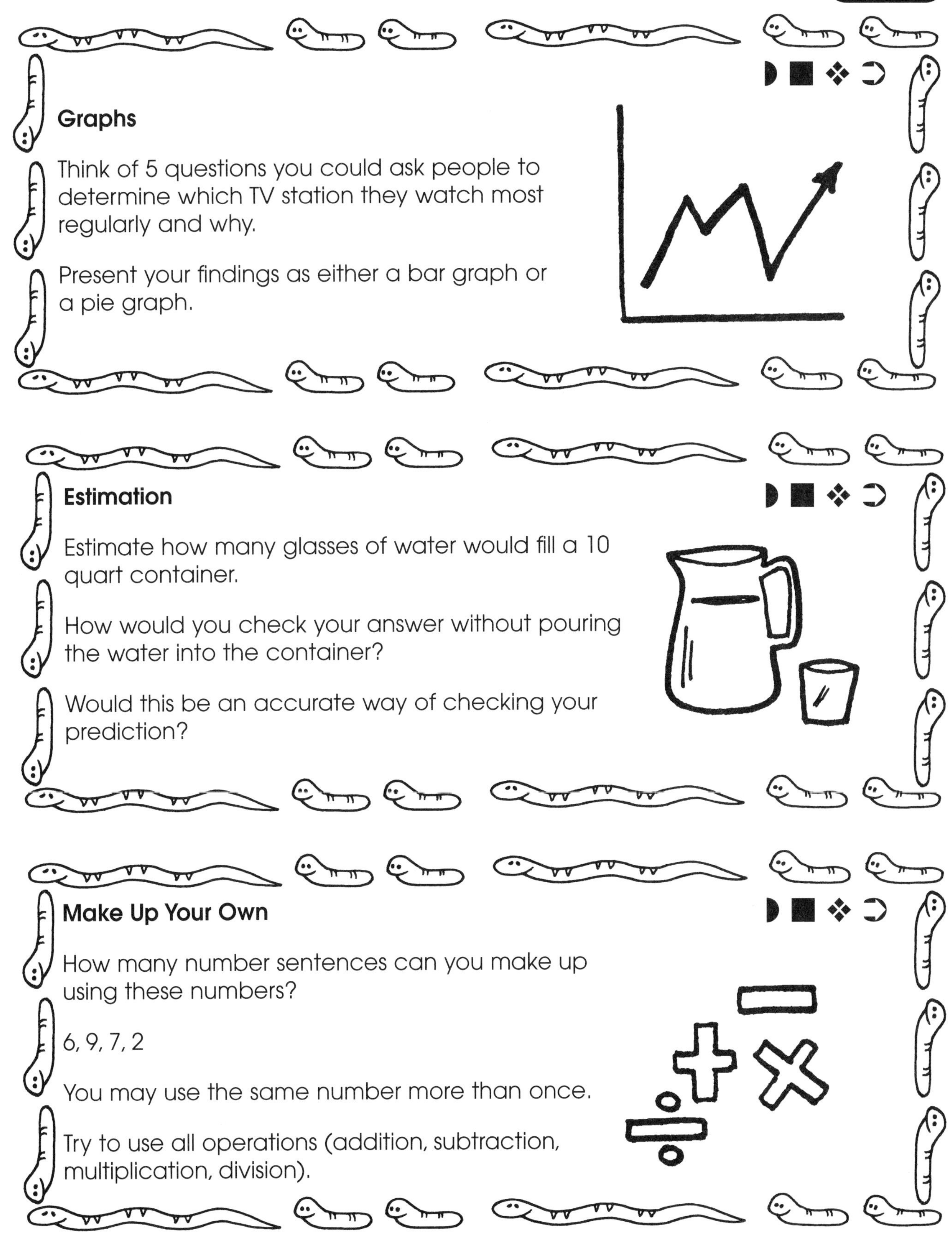

Graphs

Think of 5 questions you could ask people to determine which TV station they watch most regularly and why.

Present your findings as either a bar graph or a pie graph.

Estimation

Estimate how many glasses of water would fill a 10 quart container.

How would you check your answer without pouring the water into the container?

Would this be an accurate way of checking your prediction?

Make Up Your Own

How many number sentences can you make up using these numbers?

6, 9, 7, 2

You may use the same number more than once.

Try to use all operations (addition, subtraction, multiplication, division).

RESEARCH SKILLS | Math | TASK CARDS

Research Skills for Math

Analyzing and Synthesizing

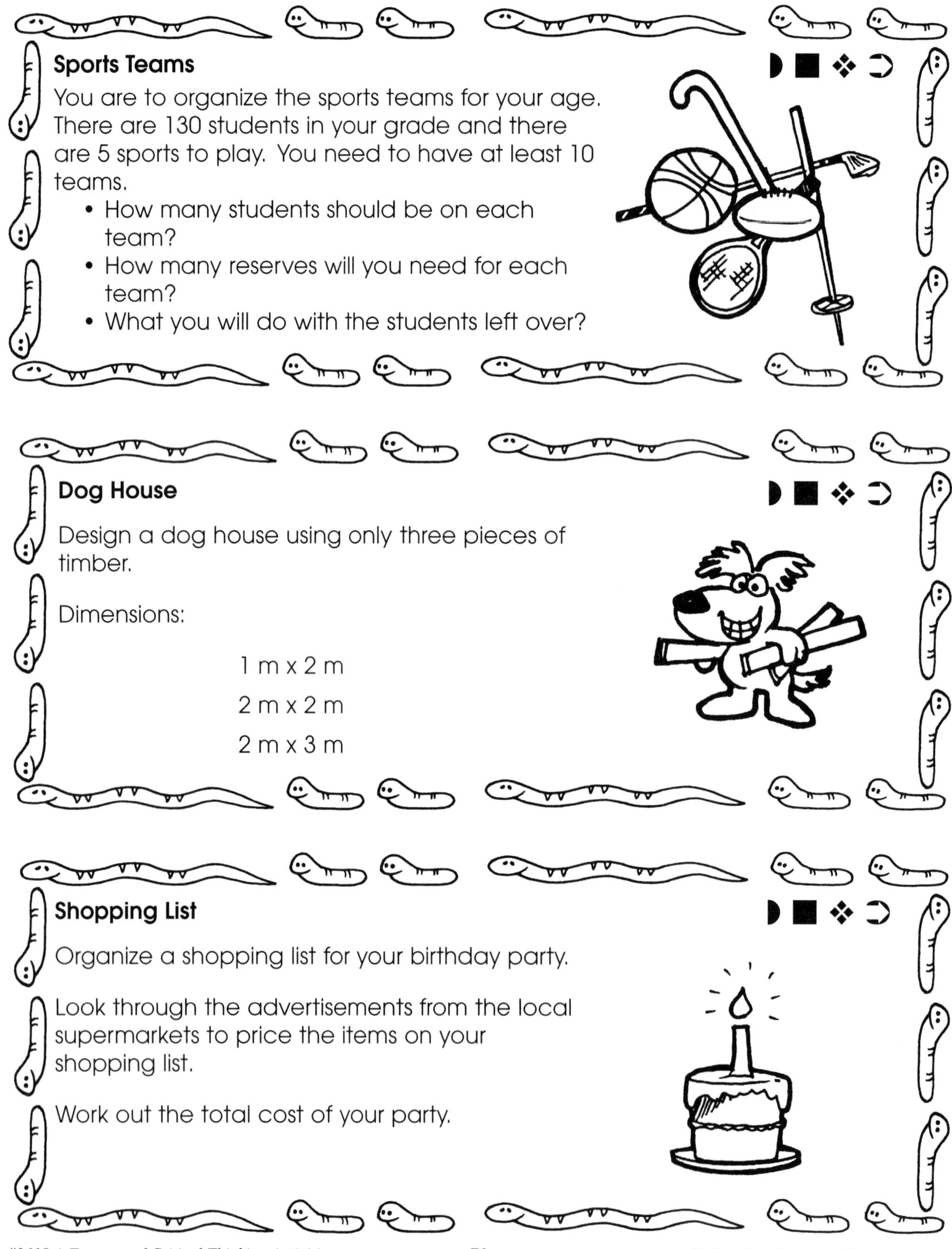

Sports Teams

You are to organize the sports teams for your age. There are 130 students in your grade and there are 5 sports to play. You need to have at least 10 teams.

- How many students should be on each team?
- How many reserves will you need for each team?
- What you will do with the students left over?

Dog House

Design a dog house using only three pieces of timber.

Dimensions:

1 m x 2 m

2 m x 2 m

2 m x 3 m

Shopping List

Organize a shopping list for your birthday party.

Look through the advertisements from the local supermarkets to price the items on your shopping list.

Work out the total cost of your party.

 © Teacher Created Materials, Inc.

Name:

Management Strategies:

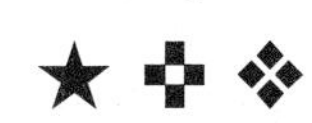

RESEARCH SKILLS

Math

BLM 24

Patterns

Sorting and Synthesizing

Design the school's new sports uniform.

You may only use 2 colors, and you must include 3 connecting shapes.

The pattern is to be repeated over the whole uniform.

The colors I have chosen are ________________ and ______________ .

Draw the 3 shapes you will use here.

My pattern will look like this:

Choose a pattern of your own.

I have decided to use ______ colors.

These will be ____

I have decided to use ______ connecting shapes.

These will be

My pattern will look like this:

RESEARCH SKILLS
Math
BLM 25

Name:

Number System

Synthesizing and Evaluating

Devise a number system to compete with the Roman numeral system.

What do the symbols look like, and what are they called?

What place value do these symbols have? (Example: v = 3)

Show what these numbers would look like in your new number system.

7	19	58
257	830	2645

Rewrite these questions using your new number system (and answer them)!

7 + 5 =	2 - 11 =
5 x 10 =	84 ÷ 7 =

© Teacher Created Materials, Inc.

Research Skills for Science

Theme: Surviving the Elements

Questioning

- Have students ask questions about the survival skills of plants, animals, and people.
  - If snakes are cold blooded, why doesn't their blood freeze in winter?
  - What do I need to keep warm?
  - How do some plants survive in the snow or in the desert?
- Encourage students to ask themselves questions to elicit prior knowledge, for example, "What did I take with me when I went camping?"
- Ask students to brainstorm "What things do we need to survive in a desert, the Arctic, the jungle?"

Planning

- Ask students to list the key words they would use to conduct an Internet search on "survival."
- Have students verbalize how they would use parts of a book such as the glossary, table of contents, and the index, to help them find information on survival.

Gathering

- Have students read stories like Sir Edmund Hilary's ascent of Everest to find out what equipment is needed to survive in extremely cold temperatures.
- Have students keep plants in different parts of the house or the classroom, such as near the window or in front of the heater. Ask them to report back on the effects and suggest ways of minimizing the effects, or finding where it grows best.

Sorting

- Ask students to sort information from the plant experiment into "things that affected growth" and "things that did not affect growth." Have students give reasons for their choices.
- Ask students to rate the above from a "very important" down to not important."
- Have students compile a survival list for a trek in the snow.

Synthesizing

- Ask students to explain the effects of heat stroke, snow blindness, or hypothermia.
- Have students work in groups of 3 or 4 to role-play life-threatening situations, such as being lost in a snowstorm in the Yukon.
- Have students create posters warning of hazards involved in mountain climbing, desert hiking or whitewater rafting.

Evaluating

- Have students explain why they wear sunscreen.
- Have students defend their inclusion of specific items in their snow trip survival list.
- Ask students to write a letter to a friend explaining what happened when they left something vital out of their survival kit.

Reporting

- Have students write a log of their journey.
- Have students present a diorama of one of the areas that they visited, for example, the snow, the desert, or the jungle.
- Have students write a television report highlighting the discovery of a new way to sustain life.

RESEARCH SKILLS

Science

BLM 26

Name:

Survival Skills

Gathering and Sorting

List all the things you would need to survive a week backpacking through the Himalayan mountains and the rain forests of the Amazon. Sort these items into the three categories below.

Himalayas	Amazon	Both

Is there anything from your list that you could do without? Why?

____

____

____

If you found yourself in a blizzard in the Himalayas, what would you do to survive?

____

____

____

Explain why you need to drink at least 2 liters of water per day while in the Amazon.

____

____

____

How could this object help you survive in the Himalayas?

____

____

____

____

 © Teacher Created Materials, Inc.

Research Skills for Social Studies

RESEARCH SKILLS
Social Studies
ACTIVITIES

Theme: Moon Colony

Questioning

- Ask students to answer open-ended questions like these:
  - Why would we want to colonize the moon?
  - How would we transport all of the things necessary to live on the moon?
  - What would we need to survive on the moon?
- Have students write down questions they would need answered before going to the moon
  - How do I breathe on the moon?
  - What does the moon surface look like?
  - How do I move around on the moon?

Planning

- Have students write down places they would locate information, for example, encyclopedias, planetariums and the Internet.
- Model a mind map so that the students have an idea of how to set out what they wish to find out.
- Show students how to access the Internet to locate information as they work in small groups.

Gathering

- Have students list things they would need to colonize the moon.
- Have students list the types of people needed to colonize the moon.
- Have them identify the skills that these people should possess.
- Have students compile a word bank of moon words.

Sorting

- Ask students to organize their information into a list of essential and non-essential skills or items.
- Have students devise a way of sorting their information according to criteria that they have identified, for example, by strength or intelligence.
- Have students sort their information into a time sequence according to what they would do first: choose the people or the equipment.
- Have students sort the moon words into different categories.

Synthesizing

- Have students explain their choices of who they would take.
- Have students decide on ways to enforce their rules and consequences.
- Ask students to present a plan of the moon settlement site.

Evaluating

- Have students write a diary of their colonization of the moon, describing high and low points.
- Ask students to list any problems they may foresee.

Reporting

- Have students write and perform a play to depict their moon colonization.
- Have students build a model of their colony using material such as clay or cardboard.
- Have students write a description of their departure and arrival on the moon.

RESEARCH SKILLS
Social Studies
BLM 27

Name: ____________________

Management Strategies:

Moon Colony

Gathering, Synthesizing, Evaluating

You have to lead a moon colonization mission. You can take seven people with you. You need to take enough food and supplies to last until you can produce more food. As the leader you need to establish some rules and consequences.

People I would include: (List professions: doctor, handyman, musician.)

	Who?	Why?
1.		
2.		
3.		
4.		
5.		

Draw and label the essential supplies you would need to take.

Write down five rules for your colony and the consequences if the rules are broken.

	Rule:	Consequence:
1.		
2.		
3.		
4.		
5.		

Follow-up Task: Construct a model of your colony. Attach labels to show where important areas such as the living quarters, storage areas, and food production sites would be.

© Teacher Created Materials, Inc.

Research Skills for Creative Arts

RESEARCH SKILLS
Creative Arts
ACTIVITIES

Theme: Redecorating Your Room

Questioning

- Have students ask themselves what they like or dislike about their bedrooms.
- Have students answer questions that make them determine the difference between needs and wants, for example, "I want a new computer" and "I need a bed to sleep on."
- Ask students to think of five questions they will be asked when they tell their parents that they want to redecorate their room.

Planning

- Have students list possible sources of information about decorating.
- Have students collect catalogs of household items, paint, and wallpaper.
- Have students draw their bedroom as it is now.

Gathering

- Ask students to find out which items could be bought second hand.
- Have students cut out pictures of different types of decorated bedrooms.
- Have students find the prices of items in catalogs and stores.

Sorting

- Have students sort the redecorating items into essential and non-essential (ones they would like to have if they could afford them).
- Have students identify a few color schemes that they would like to try.
- Ask students to organize bedroom items differently to find the best design.

Synthesizing

- Have students work out a budget for two different decorating plans.
- Ask students to decide on the items they wish to have in their rooms.
- Have students work out the budgets for their rooms, including all the changes they wish to make.

Evaluating

- Have students critically comment on their color schemes by asking questions such as: "Will it work?" "Why/Why not?"
- Ask students to prepare the case to present to their parents if their budget has gone over the allocation.
- Have students write an article for a decorating magazine describing the overall effect of their redecoration, including before and after pictures.

Reporting

- Have students make a model of their new bedroom.
- Ask students to report either orally or in written form on how they feel about their new room.
- Have students imagine they are interior decorators who must write reports about the good and bad points of redecorating a room.

RESEARCH SKILLS
Creative Arts
BLM 28

Name:

Redecorating Your Room

Management Strategies:

Gathering, Sorting, Evaluating

Your parents give you $200 to redecorate your room.

You must not make holes in any walls!

Draw a plan of how your room will look.

Floor plan of my room	Side view of my room

My color scheme:

Walls: ______________________ Curtains: ______________________

Ceiling: ______________________ Bedspread: ______________________

Other items: ____

I have chosen this color scheme because: ______________________

____

____

Budget for the cost of redecorating my room:

Item	Cost	Item	Cost
		Total Cost =	

If you go over budget with your project, what reasons would you give your parents to allow you to go ahead?

____

____

____

 © Teacher Created Materials, Inc.

Make Your Own Task Cards

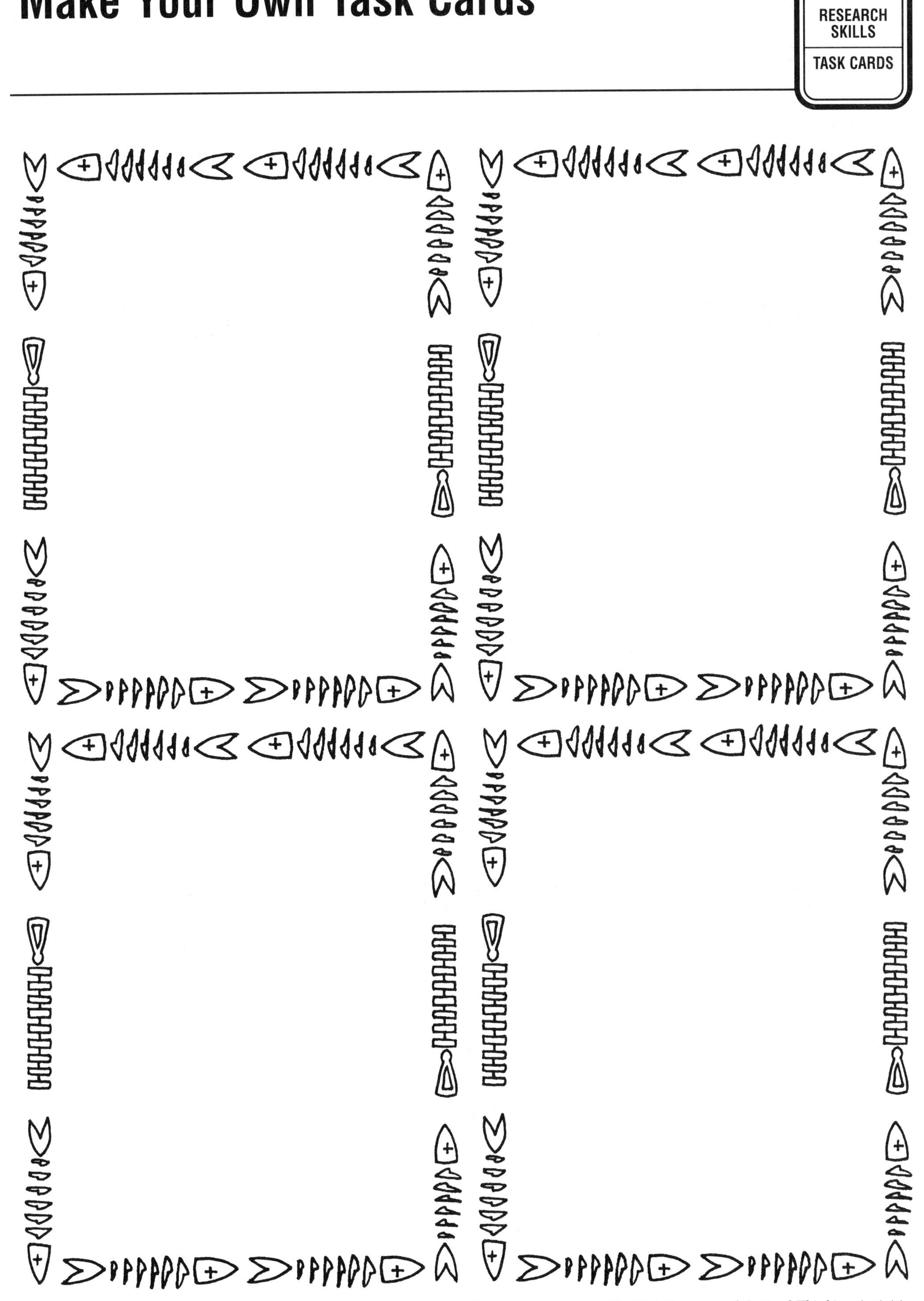

Questioning and Brainstorming Skills

Notes and Activities

by Fay Holbert

Overview for the Classroom Teacher

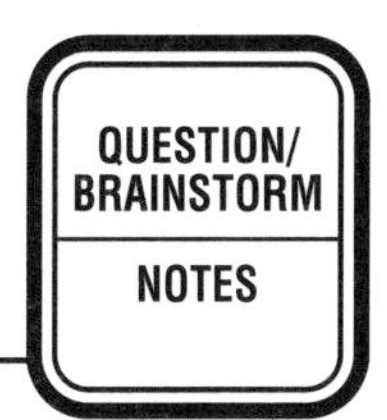

Questioning and Brainstorming Skills

Generally speaking, 30% of class time is taken up in questioning (that is about 100 questions per hour). In most classrooms 85% of questions are asked by the teacher, and 90% of those do no more than demand memory or recall by the students! Therefore, teachers should aim to use more open-ended and divergent questions to improve the students' creative thinking and problem solving abilities.

Questioning Guidelines for the Teacher:

1. Maintain a high level of enthusiasm.
2. Accept that individual differences in students will determine how, what, how much, and how fast learning occurs.
3. Encourage divergent thinking.
4. Avoid all forms of negative comments. Be positive! "Great!" "Good try!" "Tell me more!" "I've never thought of it like that!"
5. Try to minimize "Who?" "What?" "Where?" and maximize "Why?" "How?"

Bloom's taxonomy emphasizes the idea that with brighter students, more time should be devoted to the higher level activities and objectives. Knowledge and comprehension deal with facts, figures, definitions, and rules which all students need to know. However, teachers should encourage the brighter students (who will generally grasp new information quickly and comprehend more rapidly) to

- *apply* this knowledge;
- *analyze* components, relationships, and hypotheses;
- *synthesize* these components into creative solutions, plans, and theories;
- *evaluate* the accuracy, value and efficiency of alternative ideas or actions.

Examples of questions which help to apply knowledge:

When did...?
Can you list...?
Which action/event was the cause of...?
Can you give an example of...?
How would you have...?
Why was...?

Examples of questions which help to analyze knowledge:

Why did ... do this?
Can you sequence...?

Examples of questions which help to synthesize knowledge:

How would this situation have changed if...?
What if the "bears" had been "monkeys"?

Examples of questions which help to evaluate the knowledge:

How could ... have been improved?
Who do you think has the strongest character? Why?

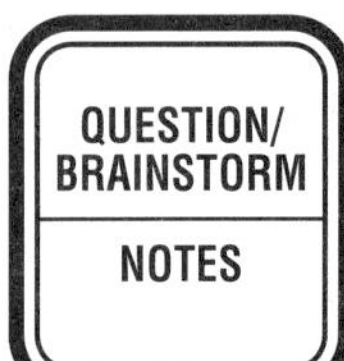

Overview for the Classroom Teacher

Brainstorming

Another technique which encourages creative thinking is **brainstorming**.

The aim of brainstorming is to develop a safe, non-judgmental setting where all students feel confident and eager to participate in the lesson.

It was Alex Osborn who identified some valuable conditions and rules for brainstorming. The main principle is deferred judgment. This means that idea evaluation is postponed until later. Osborn stressed that any kind of criticism or evaluation interferes with the generation of imaginative ideas simply because it is very difficult to do both at the same time.

It is important for the teacher to remind the students of the basic rules of brainstorming:

1. No criticism is allowed no matter how irrelevant or preposterous the responses may appear to be.
2. A large quantity of ideas is required. The more ideas you have, the more likely it is that you will have motivated all students to contribute, and thus it is more likely that you will find good solutions.
3. Accept and record all answers. To begin with, it is perhaps easier for the teacher to be the scribe, but when brainstorming is a regular feature of the class's activities, students can record responses.
4. Eliminate any stiffness or inflexibility. Be open to alternatives.
5. If responses slack off, add your own. The teacher's role is to keep urging: What else could we do? Who else has an idea? The teacher may even specifically direct questions to a group of quieter students.
6. Link ideas wherever possible. Ask questions such as "How can we express this more clearly?" "Could we improve this one?" "What if we put these three ideas together?"
7. Encourage fantasy, imagination, and lateral thinking.
8. Encourage cooperative work among students.
9. If there were a school problem (for example, the sudden appearance of graffiti on the school playground), the students could be given 24-hours notice so that all have an opportunity to discuss this at home and can be prepared to brainstorm a solution for the next day. Brighter students soon learn to organize and lead group brainstorming sessions.

Some variations of brainstorming:

Reverse brainstorming: This technique quickly points out what is currently being done incorrectly and implicitly suggests specific solutions. For example, how can we increase vandalism?

"Stop-and-Go" Brainstorming: Short periods of approximately 6 – 8 minutes of brainstorming are interspersed with evaluation. The evaluation sheets help keep the group on target by selecting the most profitable directions to pursue.

Phillips 66: This is a technique using small groups of 6. Students brainstorm for 6 minutes and then a member of each group reports the best, or all, ideas to the larger group.

 © Teacher Created Materials, Inc.

Questioning and Brainstorming for English

Theme: Famous People

Knowledge

- Pose the question: 'What does 'famous' mean to you?'
- Display photographs/magazine pictures of people who often appear in the newspapers or on television.
- Ask: "Have you ever heard of/seen any of these people on television or in newspapers? Do you consider some/any of these people to be famous?"
- Brainstorm: "Who are some famous people?" Make three lists:
  (a) Famous Local People
  (b) Famous Americans
  (c) Famous International People

Comprehension

- Ask: "What makes these people famous?" Have students provide reasons for each person's fame.
- From these responses, build up a graph on the board and have the students decide what the main reasons for fame are.
- Pose the question: "How do we decide which people are famous?"

Application

- Ask: "Do you know anyone who is famous? What makes you say this person is famous?"
- Pose the questions: "Do you know anyone that you think may become famous in the future? What are your reasons for thinking this?"
- Set up an interest center in your classroom to display books and articles about famous people from all walks of life: including sports people, musicians, politicians, diplomats, writers, scientists, humanitarians, and entrepreneurs. Encourage students to add to the collection with their own contributions.

Analysis

- From the brainstorming lists, have the students work individually or in small groups to choose one of the famous people and analyze why and how they became famous.
- Prepare a graph to show the number of famous men as compared to the number of famous women.
- Ask: "What do you notice from the graph results? What do you think the reason for this is?"

Synthesis

- Have the students write a report on one famous person of their choice. Ask them to write these first in note form and then expand it into a ten-minute oral report to present to the class.
- Pose these questions: What if your person had lived in another country, or at a different time? Might his/her story have been different? Might he/she have had a different outlook/opportunity?
- Ask: "If you could be famous for something, what would you like to be famous for?" Have students list different categories and provide reasons for their choices.

Evaluation

- Have students work in groups of four to select a famous person and decide on the high point in their chosen person's life. The group must then make up a five-minute play to show how this person reached this point.
- Have each student prepare a talk on a famous person who has most influenced their own lives. Ask them to describe how and why this happened.
- Place the original brainstorming list into categories of reasons for fame; for example, humanitarian, literature, sport, film, and music.
- Have students nominate ten people from the list that they would include in the list of The Top Ten Famous People of the Twentieth Century.

Questioning and Brainstorming Skills for English

Application and Analysis

Wall of Fame

Prepare a chart about a famous person.

Include facts, figures, and photographs.

State what you most admire about this person.

Display your chart on the "Wall of Fame" in your classroom.

Famous and Infamous

Explain the difference between "famous" and "infamous."

Give at least 5 examples of each.

Interview

Choose one of the people from your "infamous" list.

Prepare a list of questions you would ask this person in an interview.

This Is Your Life

In a small group of 4 or 5 students decide upon a famous person whom you all admire.

Prepare a "This Is Your Life" television script for this person.

 © Teacher Created Materials, Inc.

Questioning and Brainstorming Skills for English

Analysis, Synthesis, Evaluation

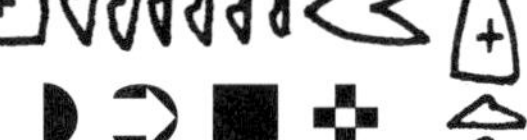

Your Choice

Interview all the members of your class. Have them all nominate one famous person for each of the categories below.

Sports	Music
Television	Movies
Medicine	Science
Politics	Writing

Is there any obvious difference between boys' and girls' opinions?

Debate

Work with two other people to prepare both sides of a debate (affirmative and negative) for this topic:

I would rather be rich than famous.

Superheroes

Superman is one "Superhero." How many others can you think of?

If you could choose one Super Hero to spend the day with, who would you choose?

What would you do?

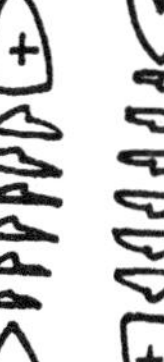

Ned Kelly

Here is the beginning of a poem written by an anonymous poet about Ned Kelly. Can you compose two more verses for it?

Ned Kelly was born in a ramshackle hut,

He'd battled since he was a kid.

He grew up with bad men, bandits and thieves

And learned all the bad things they did.

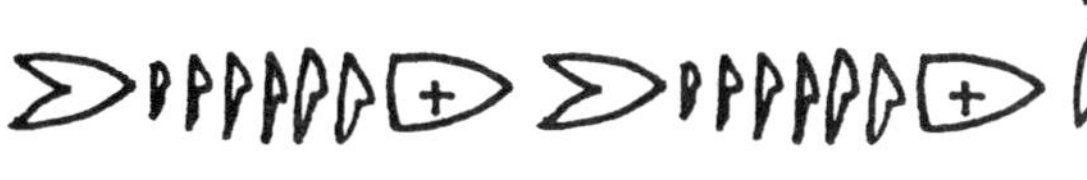

QUESTION/ BRAINSTORM
English
BLM 29

Name:

Most Famous Person

Management Strategies:

Analysis, Synthesis, Evaluation

Choose ten children and ten adults to survey. They can be from your family, or students and teachers from your school.

Ask this question: **In your opinion, who is the most famous person the world has ever known?**

Record your answers on the survey sheet below.

Person	Selection	Person	Selection

Which famous person was most popular with boys?

____

Which famous person was most popular with girls?

____

Which famous person was most popular with adults?

____

Which category was most popular? (sports, film, science, etc.)

____

Which famous person was chosen most often?

____

Using the information you have gathered, prepare a five-minute report to present to the class.

You can use graphs, overhead transparencies, models, or illustrations to help you with your presentation.

 © Teacher Created Materials, Inc.

Name:

Management Strategies:

QUESTION/ BRAINSTORM

English

BLM 30

Future Fame

Synthesis and Evaluation

Imagine that you are given the opportunity to become famous. What would you choose to be?

____

Why would you choose this?

____

____

____

Draw yourself at work.

What would you do in your new life? Where would you go? What results would you hope to achieve?

Write a diary for the first three days of being famous.

Day One: ____

____

____

Day Two: ____

____

____

Day Three: ____

____

____

Questioning and Brainstorming Skills for Math

Theme: Space — Looking at Solids

Knowledge

- Review space vocabulary—three dimensions, length, width, depth, height, sphere, cube, rectangular prism, triangular prism, pyramid, cylinder, cone.
- Ask: "What is a solid?"
- Display the seven solids discussed in vocabulary revision for identification by the students. Use more than one example of each solid in different dimensions.
- Have students group similar models together and attach flash card labels to each group of examples.
- Ask students to identify objects in the classroom which are examples of the solids nominated. Have them record responses on the board under the seven category headings.

Comprehension

- Ask: "Can you explain the difference between a shape and a solid? Why can't you carry a shape about with you?"
- Show pictures of common objects such as a hose, notebook, can of baked beans, slice of cake, ream of paper, pencil, CD case, tennis ball, ice cream, church steeple. Ask students to group like solids together.

Application

- Point out that many objects are two or more solids combined. Ask students to name which solids form these common items:

  (a) a table

  (b) a doorknob

  (c) a wine glass

  (d) a Hershey's chocolate

  (e) an ice cream cone

  (f) a chair

  (g) a church steeple

  (h) a sharpened pencil.

Analysis

- Ask students to give reasons why the six faces of a die are equal squares.
- Have students examine each of the solids on display, noting the structure of each, for example, the number and shape of each face.
- Ask: "Which common solids have sharp corners? Which ones have rounded corners? Why?"

Synthesis

Challenge the students with questions:

- Why would a one-ton sphere be easier to move than a one-ton cube?
- Why are some spheres solid and some hollow?
- Which items can you name that are solids that have been hollowed out? Why are these hollowed out solids such commonly used objects?

Evaluation

- Ask students to provide reasons why children's building blocks are usually cubes and rectangular prisms and not

  (a) triangular prisms or pyramids, or

  (b) spheres or cylinders.
- Have students use modeling clay or plasticine to construct a model of a famous building such as the Colosseum, the Eiffel Tower, or the Empire State Building. Ask them to evaluate what common solid shapes appear most in building construction.

Questioning and Brainstorming Skills for Math

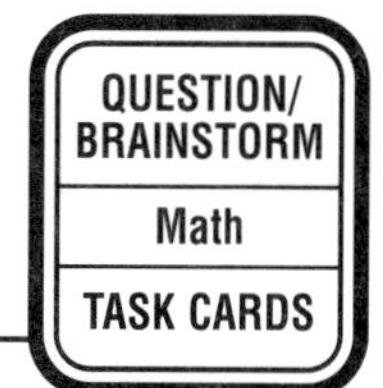

Knowledge, Comprehension, Application, Analysis

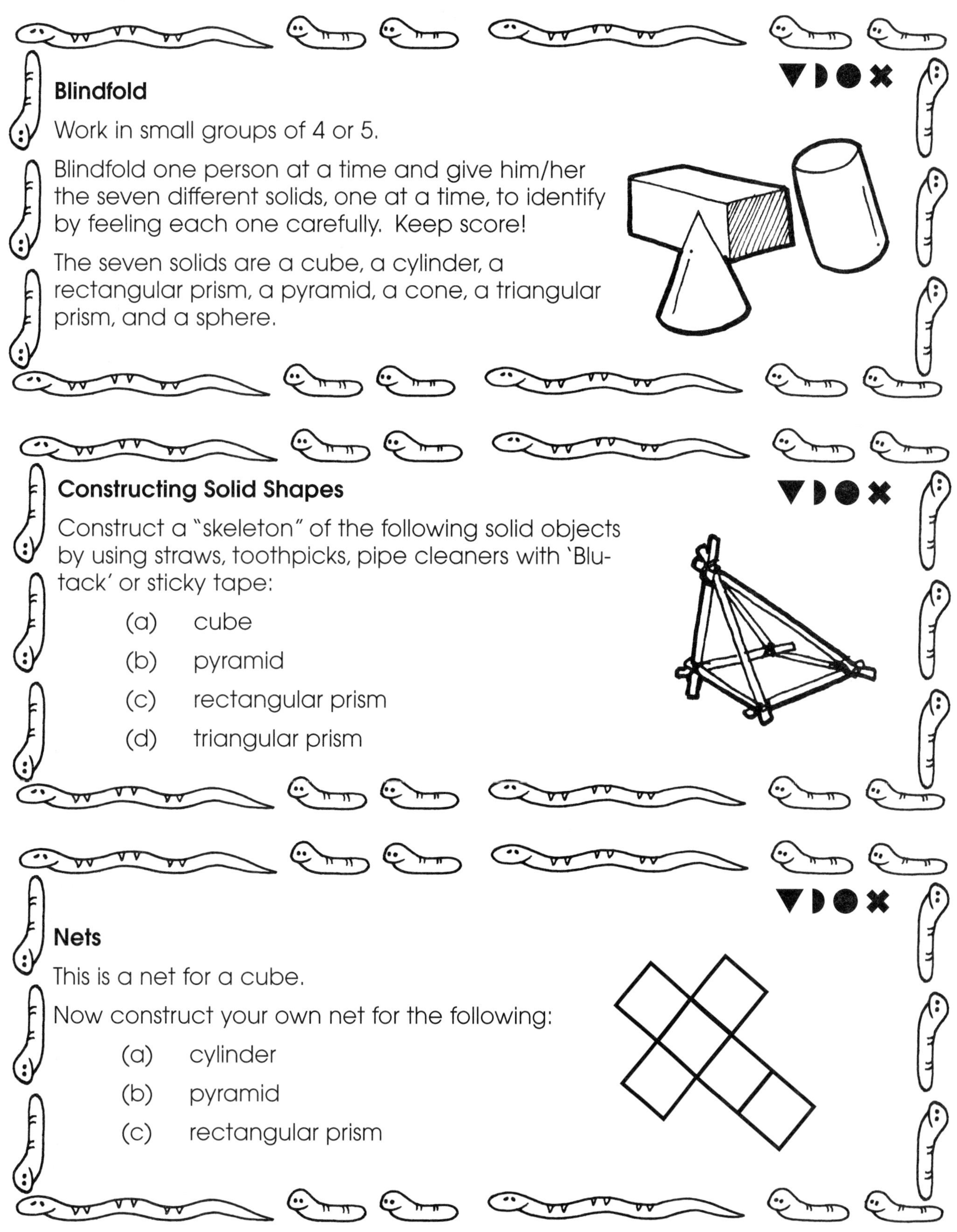

Blindfold

Work in small groups of 4 or 5.

Blindfold one person at a time and give him/her the seven different solids, one at a time, to identify by feeling each one carefully. Keep score!

The seven solids are a cube, a cylinder, a rectangular prism, a pyramid, a cone, a triangular prism, and a sphere.

Constructing Solid Shapes

Construct a "skeleton" of the following solid objects by using straws, toothpicks, pipe cleaners with 'Blu-tack' or sticky tape:

(a) cube
(b) pyramid
(c) rectangular prism
(d) triangular prism

Nets

This is a net for a cube.

Now construct your own net for the following:

(a) cylinder
(b) pyramid
(c) rectangular prism

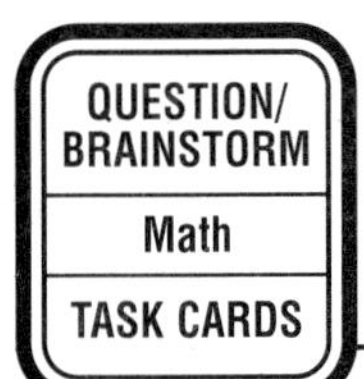

Questioning and Brainstorming Skills for Math

Comprehension, Analysis, Synthesis

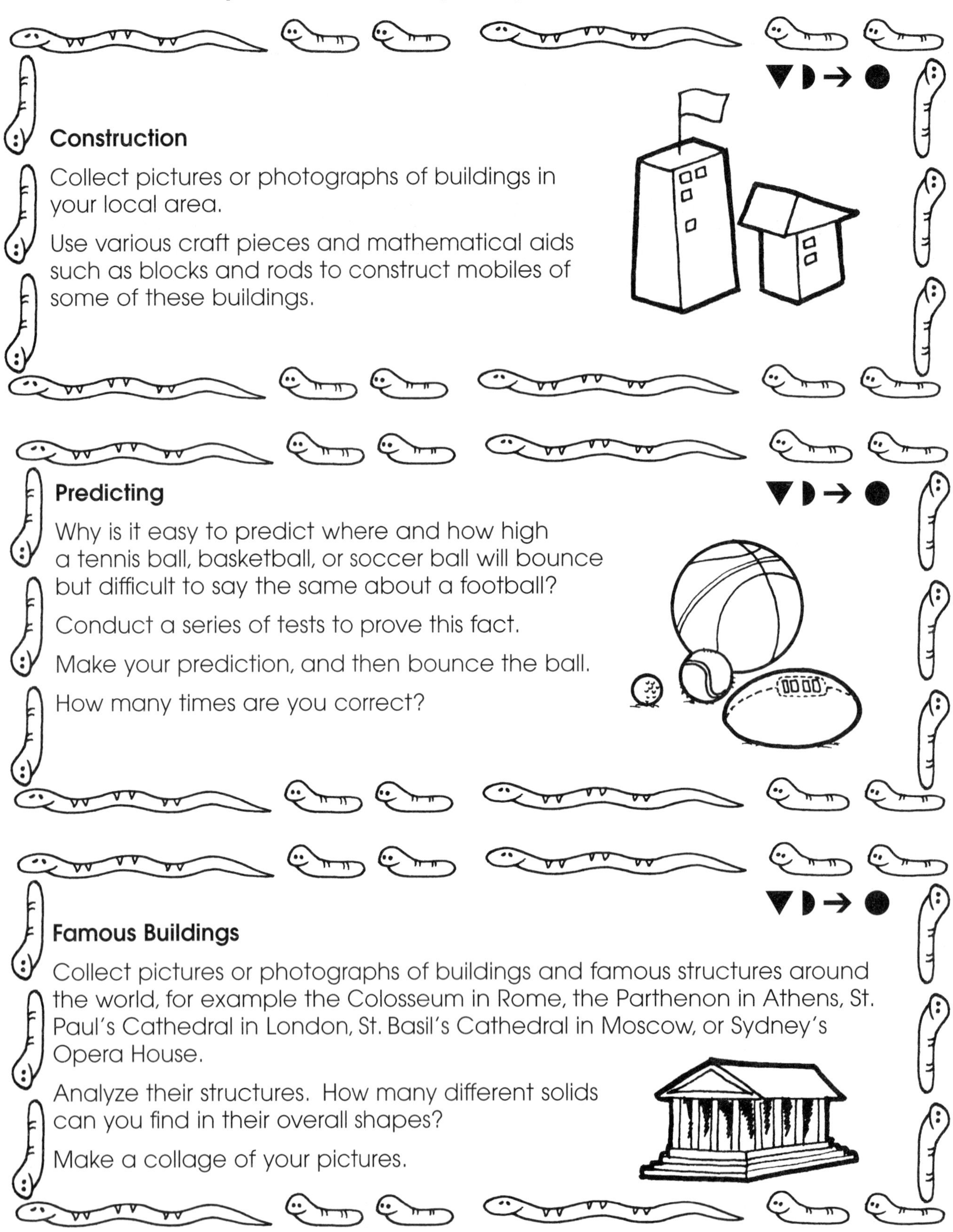

Construction

Collect pictures or photographs of buildings in your local area.

Use various craft pieces and mathematical aids such as blocks and rods to construct mobiles of some of these buildings.

Predicting

Why is it easy to predict where and how high a tennis ball, basketball, or soccer ball will bounce but difficult to say the same about a football?

Conduct a series of tests to prove this fact.

Make your prediction, and then bounce the ball.

How many times are you correct?

Famous Buildings

Collect pictures or photographs of buildings and famous structures around the world, for example the Colosseum in Rome, the Parthenon in Athens, St. Paul's Cathedral in London, St. Basil's Cathedral in Moscow, or Sydney's Opera House.

Analyze their structures. How many different solids can you find in their overall shapes?

Make a collage of your pictures.

 © Teacher Created Materials, Inc.

Name:

Management Strategies:

✶ ■ ✥ ⇛

QUESTION/ BRAINSTORM

Math

BLM 31

Looking at Solids

Analysis, Synthesis, Evaluation

Task 1: How many sports or board games can you name that use some of these solids as part of the playing equipment? Some of the boxes are filled in as an example.

Game	Cube	Rectang-ular Prism	Triangular Prism	Pyramid	Sphere	Cone	Cylinder
Basketball							
Monopoly	Dice	Money					

Task 2: Devise a team game or a board game in which at least three of the above solid shapes are used.

Name of the game: ____________________

Drawing of the equipment to be used in the game:

Description of the game: ____________________

____

____

____

QUESTION/ BRAINSTORM
Math
BLM 32

Name:

Management Strategies:

Looking at Solids

Analysis, Synthesis, Evaluation

Task: 1: Examine your seven solid shapes and fill in the following information about each one:

(a) how many faces?

(b) how many edges?

(c) how many corners?

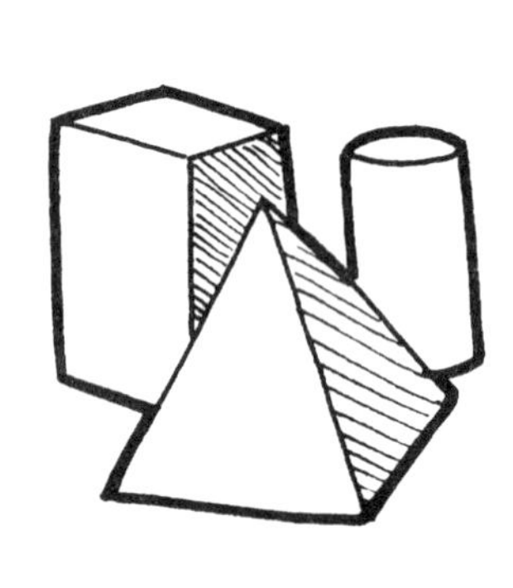

Solid Shape	Faces	Edges	Corners
Cube			
Rectangular Prism			
Triangular Prism			
Pyramid			
Sphere			
Cone			
Cylinder			

Task 2: What do you notice about the cylinder, cone, and sphere?

Task 3: Collect some containers, for example, milk, juice, yogurt, and soup. Carefully measure the length, width, and depth of each one. Using your calculator, determine the "volume" of each container.

Measurement	Milk	Juice	Yogurt	Soup
Length				
Width				
Height				
Volume				

What do you notice about your answers?

 © Teacher Created Materials, Inc.

Questioning and Brainstorming Skills for Science

Theme: Whales

Knowledge

- Brainstorm: What do you know about whales?
- Display pictures and photographs of whales. Discuss facts about their appearance, size, habitat, eating habits, and young.
- Students could work in groups of four to answer this question: How would you describe whales?

Comprehension

Pose questions:

- Where are whales to be found? Why are whales so easily killed despite their size and strength? What types of whales are there? What do whales eat? How long do whales live?
- Alternatively, challenge students to devise a list of ten fact-finding questions about whales. Then ask them to swap their list with a person near them. If any question overlaps with another on the list, cross it out. Does any student have ten questions remaining?

Application

Pose questions:

- What is different about killer whales when compared with baleen whales? Provide other groups of whales for students to compare and contrast.
- Why are people from many countries of the world involved in Save the Whale projects?
- How are whales killed? Have students compare past methods with present ones.
- How can we help to save the whales? Have students contact 'Project Jonah' at PO Box 238, North Quay, Queensland, 4002 for further ideas.

Analysis

Pose questions:

- Who are the main groups responsible for hunting whales?
- Why are these people intent on killing the whales?
- What enables whales to live in such icy waters when their body temperatures are almost identical to ours?
- Are whale numbers dropping or increasing? Why?

Synthesis

Pose question:

- What are some of the whale products which are in great demand? Could some substitutes be discovered and used? Have students design posters to advertise these substitutes. These could be placed in the school library or front foyer.
- Can you see a solution to the problem of the falling number of whales? Post solutions around the room and encourage students to add to them. Suggest a target number of solutions to reach by the end of semester.
- What would the sea be like if by 2010 there were no whales left? Write a short report for the class on this situation.

Evaluation

- Have students write to Project Jonah to recommend some actions that might help save the whales.
- Pose this question: Would it be a workable solution if a law were passed stating that there must be no more whale hunting? Why? Why not?
- Have students research how many countries have a Save the Whales organization like we have in Australia. Ask the students to find out how successful these organizations are.
- Ask: "In which countries is whaling condoned? What could be some reasons for this?"

QUESTION/ BRAINSTORM
Science
TASK CARDS

Questioning and Brainstorming Skills for Science

Application and Synthesis

Whaling

On a map of the world, use different colors to show the following:

- where the major whaling areas are found
- which nations are responsible for most of the whale hunting
- which whales are hunted

Save the Whale

If you were a scientist, how could you minimize the killing of whales?

Television Commercial

Devise a publicity campaign to help save the whale.

Write the script for a short television commercial that puts forward an argument that would help to save the whales.

Select the cast to dramatize this commercial.

Design a persuasive poster to follow up the commercial.

Did You Know?

Did you know that whales were used in the Vietnam War?

See if you can find out why? where? how?

How do you feel about using whales this way?

Name:

Management Strategies:

QUESTION/ BRAINSTORM

Science

BLM 33

Whales

Analysis, Synthesis, Evaluation

Task 1: Research the correct measurements of an adult blue whale.

Task 2: Using these measurements, use colorful streamers to create a life-size outline of a Blue Whale on your school playground.

Task 3: Can you estimate and then work out the following:

(a) How many children of your age would fit into a Blue Whale?

Estimation: ____________ Actual Number: ____________

(b) How many small cars would be the same weight and length as a blue whale?

Estimation: ____________ Actual Number: ____________

How did you calculate these?

(a)____

(b)____

Task 4: Draw a blue whale and its calf in the box below.

How often does a whale have calves?

____

How long does the mother whale feed her babies?

____

Task 5: Whales are mammals. What does this mean?

____

Name some other mammals:

____

____

____

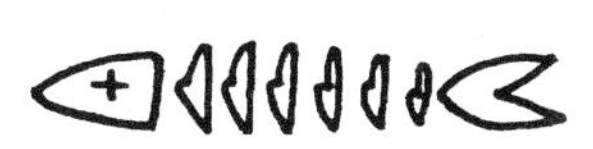

Questioning and Brainstorming Skills for Social Studies

Theme: Hobbies and Pastimes

Knowledge

Brainstorm the following topics:

- What is your favorite hobby or pastime?
- Who can have a hobby or pastime?
- What are some hobbies or pastimes that your parents have?
- Why do people have hobbies or pastimes?

Comprehension

Pose these questions:

- Who should choose your hobby or pastime? Why?
- How long have you had your present hobby or pastime?
- Are hobbies very expensive?
- Should people have both an indoor and an outdoor hobby or pastime?

Application

- Ask students to think about the personal benefits of having a hobby or pastime.
- Have students identify what attracted them to their present hobby.
- Ask students how many different hobbies they have had since they started school. Have them identify reasons for the changes.
- Ask: "Does your hobby or pastime help you in any way with your school work?"

Analysis

- Have students brainstorm the following topics:

  Which hobbies can be dangerous?

  In which hobbies do you participate by yourself?

  In which hobbies do you participate in a group?
- Ask: "How do hobbies and pastimes benefit people generally?"
- Ask: "When do you participate in your hobby or pastime?"

Synthesis

- Have students describe ways in which hobbies can make money.
- Ask students to describe how a hobby could eventually develop into an occupation. Have them research cases of famous people where this has happened, for example, Bill Gates and technology.
- Have students work with a partner to devise ways in which their present hobbies could earn them money.

Evaluation

Pose these questions:

- By practicing, can you improve your skills in your hobby/pastime? Have students identify which skills they would need to practice.
- Do you need someone to guide you in your hobby or pastime? Why?
- Where can you find mentors to help you? Follow this up by contacting suitable people in the community who could come to speak to the class about their own hobbies. They could speak to the class as a whole and then later in greater depth to a small group particularly interested in that hobby.

 © Teacher Created Materials, Inc.

Name:

Management Strategies:

▼ ✶ ● ⊃

QUESTION/ BRAINSTORM

Social Studies

BLM 34

Hobbies

Analysis, Synthesis, Evaluation

Task 1: List five hobbies for which you would require the following skills:

Physical Strength

Coordination

Creative Thinking

Task 2: Can you recommend a hobby for these students?

Type of Student	Recommended Hobby	Why Recommended
Physically Impaired		
Visually Impaired		
Hearing Impaired		
Inner-City Dweller		
Rural Dweller		
Extremely Shy Loner		

Task 3: Describe the strangest hobby you know about.

Questioning and Brainstorming Skills for Social Studies

Comprehension, Analysis, Synthesis

Make Your Own Task Cards

Renzulli's Enrichment Triad Notes and Activities

by Rosalind Curtis

 © Teacher Created Materials, Inc.

Overview for the Classroom Teacher

Introduction to Renzulli's Enrichment Triad Model

The Enrichment Triad Model was devised by Joseph Renzulli in 1983 as a framework to provide students with the skills to carry out their own research investigations. Renzulli believes that all students should be given the opportunity to develop higher order thinking skills and pursue enriched high-end learning.

When implementing the Enrichment Triad Model in the classroom, the teacher's priority is the development of independence and encouragement of self-directed learning. The open-endedness of this model gives students the freedom to make choices about topics, resources, and manner of presentation. Teachers will also find a freedom in structure that allows them to guide their students through investigations and projects step by step, while still being able to change the process to suit the needs of individual students.

The Three Types of Activities

There are three types of activities within the Triad Model. They are the following:

Type I — exploratory experiences. Students' interests are identified. Students are given the opportunity to explore something new and extend their learning within a familiar topic.

Type II — group training activities. These activities promote the development of thinking and feeling processes with a major focus on advanced levels of thinking. These activities provide students with the necessary skills to carry out individual and small group investigations and include the following:

- creative and critical thinking skills
- decision making
- problem solving
- communication skills, and
- research skills.

These activities develop "learning how to learn" skills. They focus on

- becoming more creative
- research techniques, and
- how to use different types of equipment.

Type III — individual and/or small group investigations of real issues. Students use appropriate methods of research and inquiry and develop management plans to aid in completion of the investigation.

Type I and II enrichment activities provide the basic skills needed for students to carry out their own or group investigations. Type III enrichment activities require a high level of commitment from the students and actively engage them in the learning process by expecting them to add new knowledge, ideas, or products to a field of study. (**Note**: Ensure that students have participated in Type I and Type II activities before embarking on a Type III activity.)

All three types of enrichment activities are interrelated to a high degree within the model. The diagram below illustrates this interrelation.

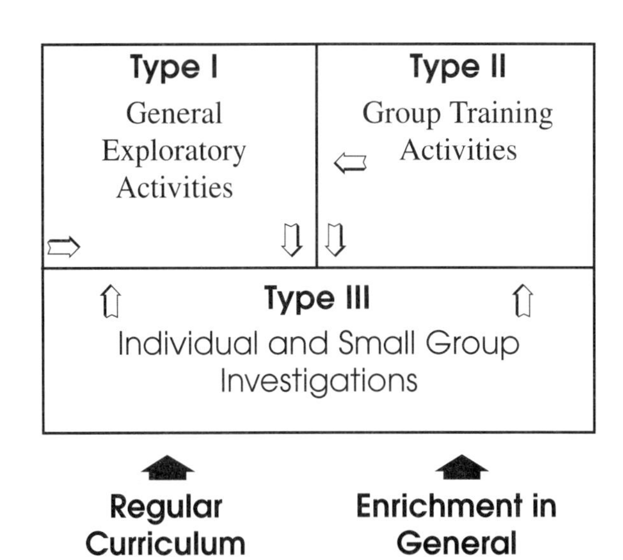

Overview for the Classroom Teacher

Classroom Management

The Enrichment Triad Model emphasizes high quality outcomes for students that reflect the amount of understanding and the depth of thought of participating students. Depending upon ability in relation to the task at hand, students may start at any point within the model; however, allowing students to embark on Type III activities without background knowledge and training (Type I and II activities) may result in a poor or less than worthwhile investigation.

Type I

Students need to be given freedom to explore a variety of topics. This exploration must be purposeful and students must come up with some ideas for what they would like to study and how they will go about this.

For example, student may be interested in insects. The student then looks at material related to insects and develops questions to be investigated. These may include the following:

- Why do insects only have six legs?
- Do all insects have the same body structure?
- What does an insect do?

The student will also come up with a plan to find the information to answer these questions. For example the student might:

- interview the curator at a local museum
- find and observe insects in their natural habitat

Teachers need to help students identify areas of study and stimulate their interest. To start the process, ask students to talk about their interests. Once a student has identified an area of interest, the teacher needs to keep checking on progress by holding formal and informal meetings to discuss findings.

Type I activities should assist the teacher to decide which Type II activities need to be taught to particular groups of students.

Type II

As these activities are training exercises to help the student deal more effectively with finding content, the teacher must ensure that the skills are first taught in a content-free lesson. Once the skills are internalized, the student can apply them to a specific task.

These skills focus on critical analysis, problem solving, and divergent and creative thinking.

Type III

Not all students pursue an individual or small group investigation for every topic. Type III enrichment activities are designed to do the following:

- foster a desire to find out more about a topic of interest
- provide an opportunity for those students who have shown interest, willingness, and commitment to carry out an investigation of their own
- actively engage students in the formulation of a real issue and decision about a plan of action, and
- encourage students to produce new information for their topic and to present their findings to audiences for whom there is some relevance

 © Teacher Created Materials, Inc.

Renzulli's Enrichment Triad for English

RENZULLI'S TRIAD
English
ACTIVITIES

General

- Activities need to be provided that are additional to the regular curriculum and provide enrichment and extension.
- Ensure that most enrichment activities are Type III activities.
- Where necessary, provide opportunities for students to attend higher grades to participate in curriculum extension work.
- Arrange for students to work with mentors from within the school community or from the local area.
- Take into account students' specific content interests and learning styles.
- Ensure that Type I activities involve little structure, but give some idea as to the type of investigation to be undertaken.

Type I

- Conduct brainstorming sessions to gain knowledge of students' interests for investigation.
- Arrange appropriate guest speakers to talk with the students about their area of expertise.
- Create learning centers. Provide various sources from related fields of study to stimulate interest and the desire to learn more.
- Organize field trips to places of interest where the students will be enticed to follow investigations of their own.

Type II

- Students complete basic research projects where they are required to develop research and reporting skills. Some project examples include the following:
  - Why do dogs have fur?
  - How do ships float?
- Encourage students to complete small-scale investigations related to a central theme. These should require them to develop such skills as collecting and recording data and reporting on it. For example:
  - Choose two different types of snakes and compare their prey, predators, and methods of killing and defense.
  - Compare helicopters and fixed-wing airplanes.
- Help students develop problem solving strategies. Ask questions that require problem identification for actions. For example:
  - If all of the trees in the world were destroyed, what would our world be like?
- Ask students to complete a well-defined research topic.

Type III

- Actively involve students in formulating the issue they wish to investigate.
- Ensure that the students have chosen a topic of personal interest and have a genuine desire to find out more about it.
- Hold regular meetings to check student progress—time frame and goals.
- At the end of their investigations, students produce new information in various media. For example:
  - an article for a magazine
  - a video.

RENZULLI'S TRIAD
English
BLM 35

Name:

Management Strategies:

Type II – Helicopters

1. On a separate sheet of paper:

   Draw a helicopter. Label it.

   Draw a fixed wing aircraft. Label it.

2. List ways in which helicopters and planes are used to help people.

Helicopters	Planes

3. Describe how helicopters take off. What is the main difference between helicopters and planes in their take off procedures?

4. Which aircraft would be more suitable in these situations. Explain why you think so.

transporting workers to an off-shore oil rig	herding cattle
taking a concert group to another state to perform	taking people in a parachuting contest to the drop-off point

 © Teacher Created Materials, Inc.

Name:

Management Strategies:

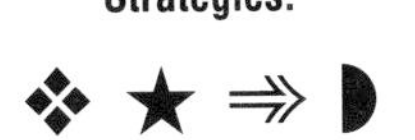

RENZULLI'S TRIAD
English
BLM 36

Type II – Biography of an Outlaw

1. Form a group of four and choose a outlaw as the subject of a biography.
2. Brainstorm all you know about the outlaw. With this information, complete the mind map below:

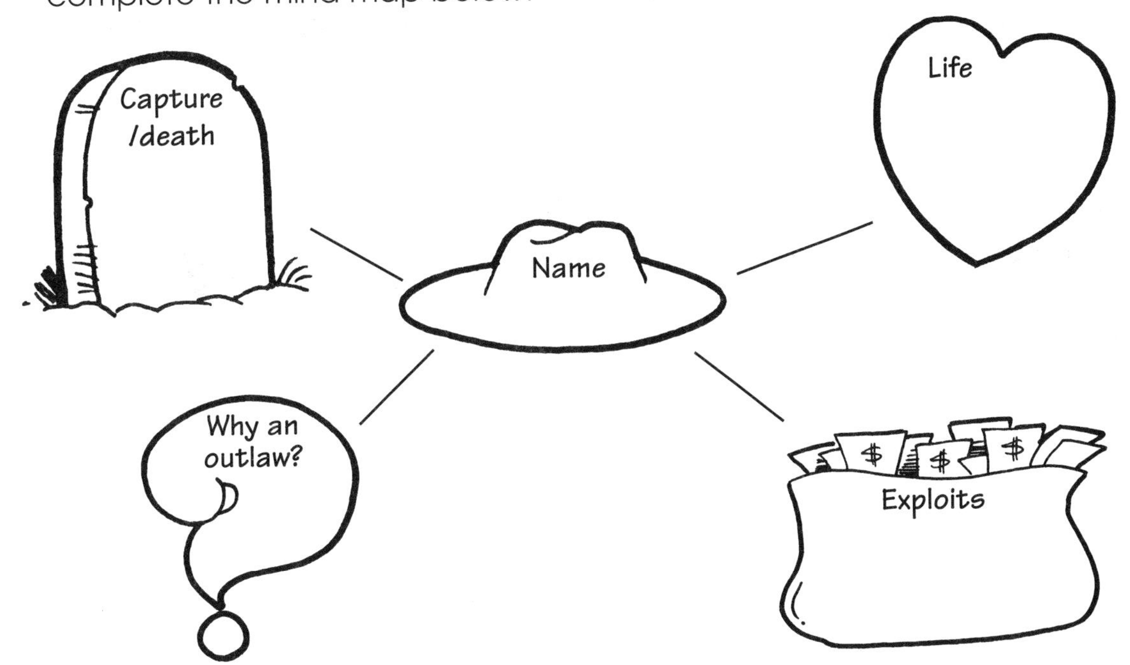

3. Look at the information. Write down what else you need to know to introduce your outlaw.

______________________ ______________________
______________________ ______________________
______________________ ______________________

4. Using one source only, find the answers to your questions. Take note of how your outlaw dressed.
5. On a large piece of cardboard or paper, trace around one member of your group. Use this shape as a model of the outlaw. Dress the model in the clothes of the day.
6. Using your model and all the information you have gathered, prepare an introduction to this outlaw. Present the outlaw to the rest of the class, telling of his life.

RENZULLI'S TRIAD
English
TASK CARDS

Renzulli's Enrichment Traid for English

Theme: Zoo Visit—Mammals

Type I

All about Mammals

On your visit to the zoo, write down the names of all the mammals you see.

Ask the handler of these animals why they are classified as mammals.

Choose one mammal and write down five things you would like to find out about it.

Type II

Endangered Species

In a group of four or five, discuss the questions below. Give as many solutions as you can:

1. How can we save endangered mammals for future generations?
2. How can we minimize the effects of human habitation on these mammals?
3. What would you do if we were the endangered species?

Type II

Model Habitat

With a friend, choose one of the mammals you saw at the zoo and make a diorama that does the following:

- depicts the mammal's habitat
- shows its prey
- shows how it avoids its predators, and
- shows how it cohabits with humans (if it does)

Type III

Wildlife Warrior

Identify an issue related to a particular endangered animal.

Make a plan of how you would investigate ways to lessen the impact of this issue on the animal.

Explain how you would let the world know of your plan to save the animal.

© Teacher Created Materials, Inc.

Renzulli's Enrichment Triad for English

RENZULLI'S TRIAD
English
TASK CARDS

Theme: Sport

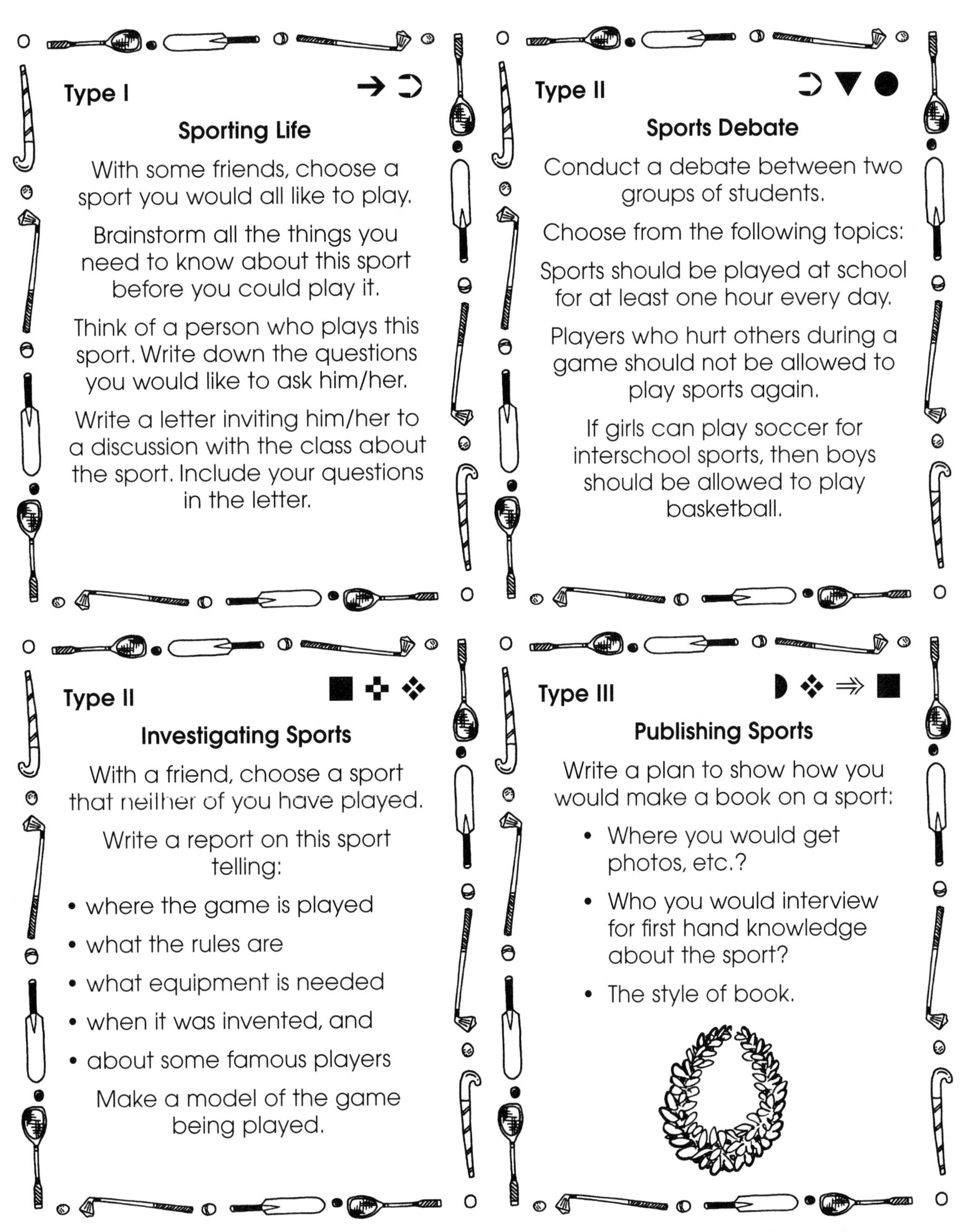

Type I

➔ ⊃

Sporting Life

With some friends, choose a sport you would all like to play.

Brainstorm all the things you need to know about this sport before you could play it.

Think of a person who plays this sport. Write down the questions you would like to ask him/her.

Write a letter inviting him/her to a discussion with the class about the sport. Include your questions in the letter.

Type II

⊃ ▼ ●

Sports Debate

Conduct a debate between two groups of students.

Choose from the following topics:

Sports should be played at school for at least one hour every day.

Players who hurt others during a game should not be allowed to play sports again.

If girls can play soccer for interschool sports, then boys should be allowed to play basketball.

Type II

■ ✜ ❖

Investigating Sports

With a friend, choose a sport that neither of you have played.

Write a report on this sport telling:

- where the game is played
- what the rules are
- what equipment is needed
- when it was invented, and
- about some famous players

Make a model of the game being played.

Type III

◗ ❖ ⇛ ■

Publishing Sports

Write a plan to show how you would make a book on a sport:

- Where you would get photos, etc.?
- Who you would interview for first hand knowledge about the sport?
- The style of book.

RENZULLI'S TRAID

Math

ACTIVITIES

Renzulli's Enrichment Triad for Math

General

- Ensure that mastery in all basic competencies is made efficiently and rapidly.
- Arrange realistic contracts with students.
- Develop concepts in all areas of math through sequential developmental instruction.
- Develop skill centers where students apply and extend particular skills (addition, subtraction, multiplication, division, problem solving) in real-life situations.
- Provide games for students that apply learned skills and use logic to solve problems.
- Provide hands-on material for students to help develop concepts and ideas.

Type I

- Ask students to arrange counters, blocks, or buttons into as many different patterns as possible for given numbers. For example:

  14 can be arranged these ways

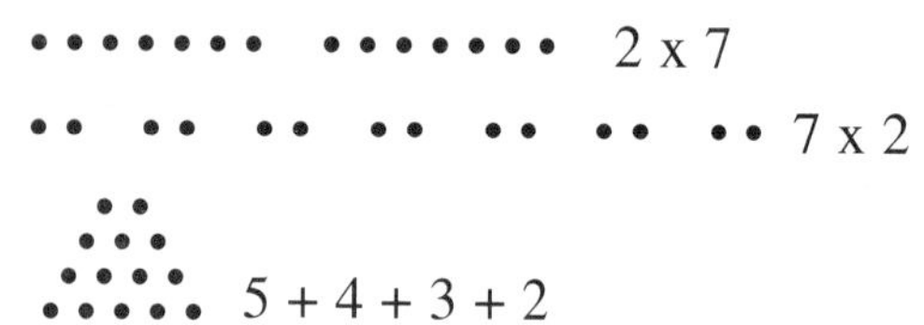

- Ask students to list known mathematical terms and how they can be described or used. For example:
  - Subtraction makes numbers smaller.
  - Fraction—a part of a whole.
- Brainstorm as many possible ways to complete an algorithm, for example, using the numbers 20, 5, 15, make up as many number sentences as possible that are true: 20 = 5 + 15, 20 > 5 < 15, 20 – 15 = 5.
- Organize for a professional to talk to students about the importance of math in their daily work. For example, a chef can talk about the importance of fractions in cooking.

Type II

- Ask students to prepare graphs of information from surveys they have taken. Report their findings to the class.
- Ask students to predict weights and measurements of objects by using arbitrary units. For example, use fingers to measure length. Let them check that the predictions are accurate.
- Ask students to solve mathematical problems, using a combination of operations. For example:
  - A school has 12 classes of 30 students. If one third of the students attend the school choir performance, how many children are left at school?
- Ask students to analyze a problem and to come up with different solutions.

Type III

- Encourage students to state an hypothesis before starting an investigation.
- Ask students to predict findings prior to beginning a project and, on completion, to check the accuracy of the predictions.
- Assist students as they develop plans to carry out their investigations that including methods to be used and the intended audience.
- Allow opportunities for students to present their findings to their intended audience in as many different ways as possible—pictorially, orally, through use of computers, or as a written report.

 © Teacher Created Materials, Inc.

Name:

RENZULLI'S TRIAD
Math
BLM 37

Type I and II—Fractions

1. Look through cookbooks and list, in the following categories, all the measurements that are mentioned.

Whole spoons	Parts of spoons	Whole cups	Parts of cups
other measurements			

2. Look through other books (e.g., nature, history, science, fiction) and write down any fractions that are mentioned. Sort them into these categories:

Time	Percentage	Length	Weight	Part of numbers

3. List some people who use fractions daily in their jobs. How would knowing how to work with fractions help these people in their jobs?

Jobs that use fractions	How fractions make these jobs easier

(Use the back of this sheet if necessary.)

RENZULLI'S TRIAD
Math
BLM 38

Name:

Management Strategies:

Type II—Money: Small-Scale Investigation

1. Find out the monetary unit for these countries:

Australia Indonesia England France Russia Fiji

2. Look in the newspaper to find out what the United States dollar is worth in these countries.

Australia	Indonesia	England
France	Russia	Jamica

3. Survey your class to find out how much pocket money they receive, what they spend it on and how often they receive it.

   Record the questions you will ask below:

4. Record your findings in 3 different ways. (You can do this on the back of this paper or on another paper.) First, list the methods you'll use:

Method 1	Method 2	Method 3

5. Make 4 statements about your findings:

6. Looking at the monetary units from other countries and their values compared to the United States dollar, what can you say about your friends' pocket money?

 © Teacher Created Materials, Inc.

Renzulli's Enrichment Triad for Math

RENZULLI'S TRIAD
Math
TASK CARDS

Theme: Time

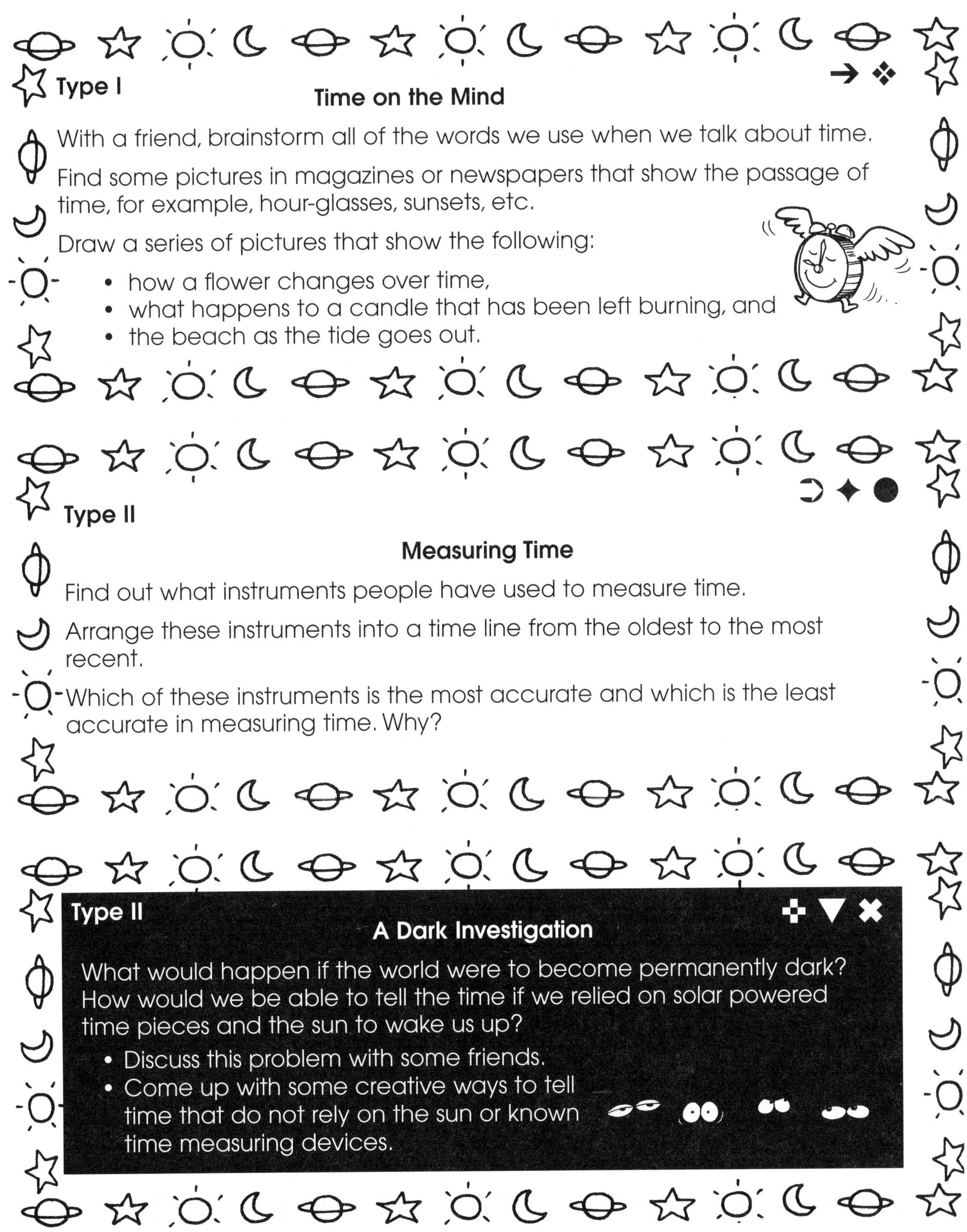

Type I

Time on the Mind

With a friend, brainstorm all of the words we use when we talk about time.

Find some pictures in magazines or newspapers that show the passage of time, for example, hour-glasses, sunsets, etc.

Draw a series of pictures that show the following:

- how a flower changes over time,
- what happens to a candle that has been left burning, and
- the beach as the tide goes out.

Type II

Measuring Time

Find out what instruments people have used to measure time.

Arrange these instruments into a time line from the oldest to the most recent.

Which of these instruments is the most accurate and which is the least accurate in measuring time. Why?

Type II

A Dark Investigation

What would happen if the world were to become permanently dark? How would we be able to tell the time if we relied on solar powered time pieces and the sun to wake us up?

- Discuss this problem with some friends.
- Come up with some creative ways to tell time that do not rely on the sun or known time measuring devices.

© Teacher Created Materials, Inc.

RENZULLI'S TRIAD
Math
TASK CARDS

Renzulli's Enrichment Traid for Math

Theme: Area

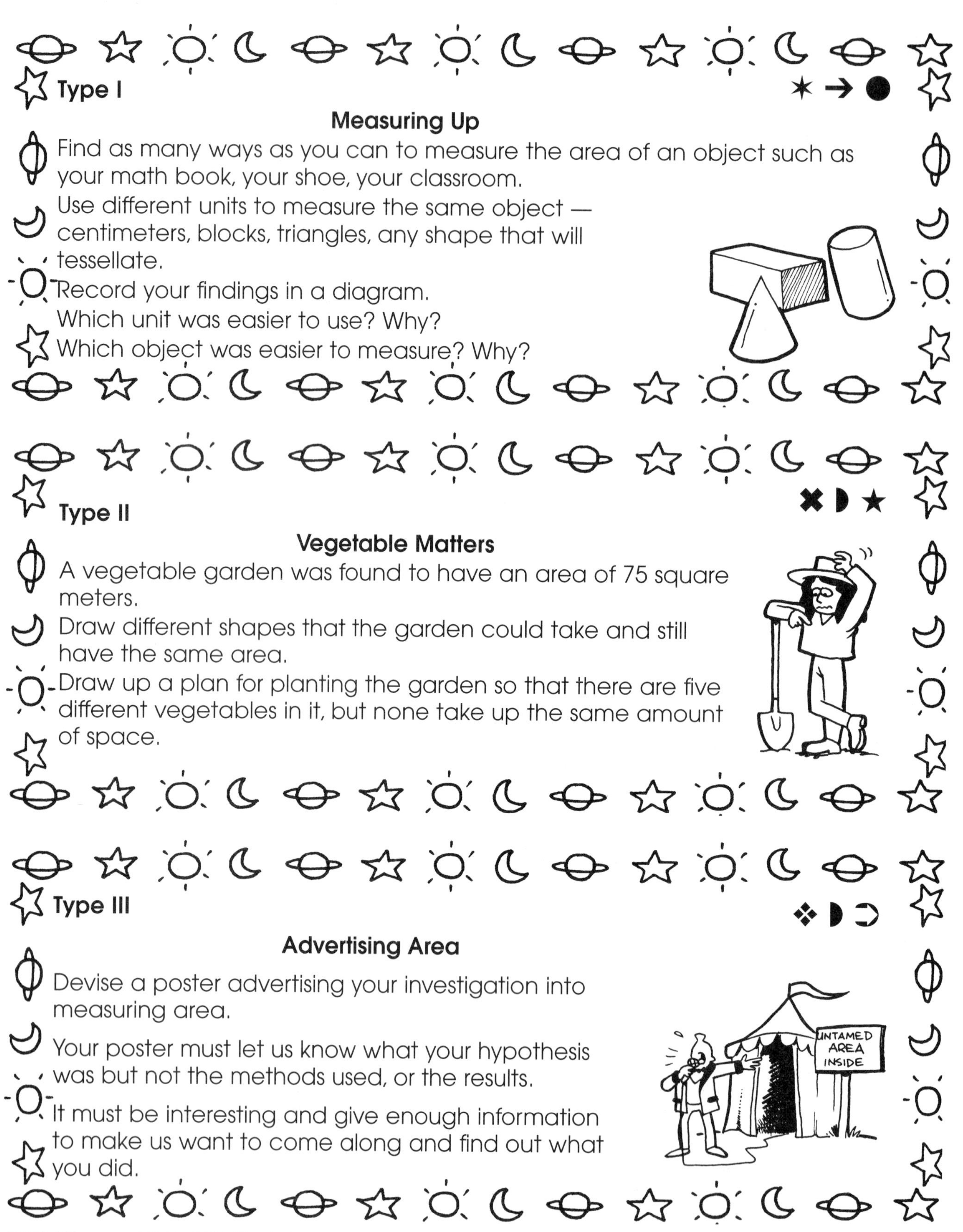

Type I

Measuring Up

Find as many ways as you can to measure the area of an object such as your math book, your shoe, your classroom.

Use different units to measure the same object — centimeters, blocks, triangles, any shape that will tessellate.

Record your findings in a diagram.

Which unit was easier to use? Why?

Which object was easier to measure? Why?

Type II

Vegetable Matters

A vegetable garden was found to have an area of 75 square meters.

Draw different shapes that the garden could take and still have the same area.

Draw up a plan for planting the garden so that there are five different vegetables in it, but none take up the same amount of space.

Type III

Advertising Area

Devise a poster advertising your investigation into measuring area.

Your poster must let us know what your hypothesis was but not the methods used, or the results.

It must be interesting and give enough information to make us want to come along and find out what you did.

Renzulli's Enrichment Triad for Science

RENZULLI'S TRIAD
Science
ACTIVITIES

General

- Develop learning centers that integrate science across the curriculum.
- Create interest centers devoted to different areas of science such as geology, chemistry, ecology, famous scientists, astronomy, etc.
- Encourage students to look at problems creatively and to come up with many possible solutions.
- Before allowing students to embark on Type III activities, ensure that scientific terms and concepts are understood. This can be achieved by ensuring that the curriculum is presented in an interesting and developmental manner.
- Allow students to question what they see.

Type I

- Create mixed-media learning/interest centers that include hands-on materials about themes or particular phenomena such as earthquakes, cyclones, animal life cycles, planets or outer space, air travel, etc. Ask students to bring in material about a subject that they enjoy to add to this list.
- Brainstorm areas of interest with students and group them according to their preferences.
- Do simple experiments with the students and ask them to write down what they observe and why they think it happened.

Type II

- Ask students to answer questions that encourage divergent thinking. For example:
  - If you had to do without one of your senses, which would it be and how would you get on without it?
  - List things that grow.
  - How many experiments can you create using two magnets?
- Organize experiments that require students to collect, record, and communicate their findings. For example, looking at individual differences, record the following data for a number of different peers:
  - Catch a ball for one minute and record how many times it can be done.
  - Record how many breaths it takes to blow up and burst a balloon.
  - Record who can touch their noses with their tongues.
  - Record who can jump furthest from a standing start with two feet together.
- Ask students to watch videos about natural disasters and write down what they observe before, during, and after the event.
- With students, devise research topics that help them to develop questioning and information gathering techniques.

Type III

- Ask students their reasons for their investigations. Their answers should reflect their personal desires to find out more about the topics.
- Ask students to write out their investigation plans. Provide help from mentors, peer tutors, parents, or other resources where necessary.
- Conduct a science fair so that students can present the findings of their investigations.

RENZULLI'S TRIAD | Science | BLM 39

Name:

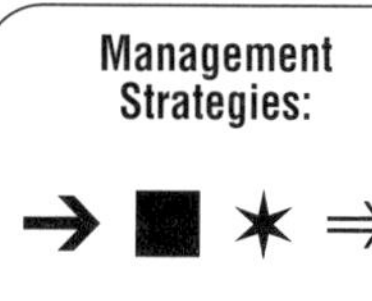

Type I—Observations

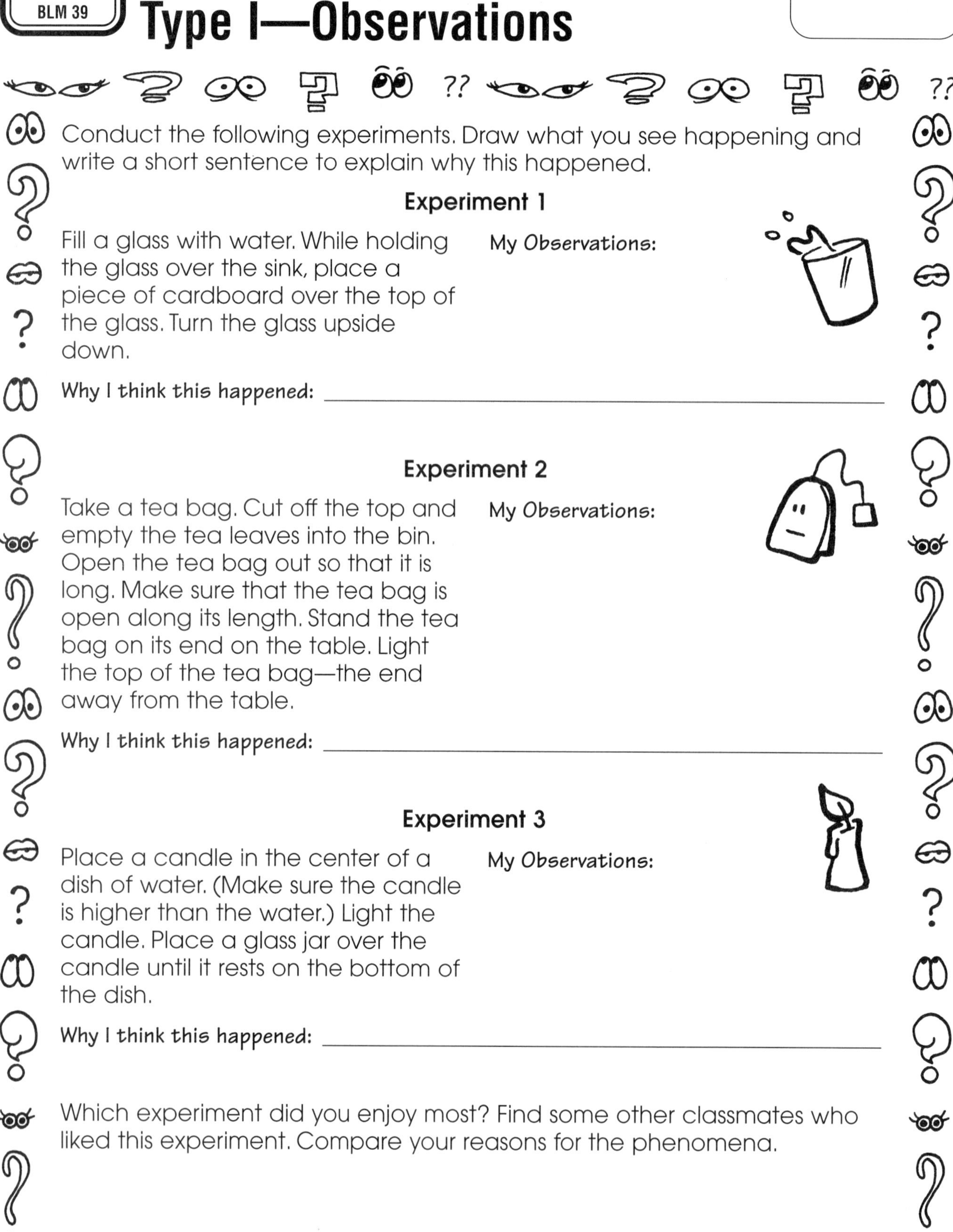

Conduct the following experiments. Draw what you see happening and write a short sentence to explain why this happened.

Experiment 1

Fill a glass with water. While holding the glass over the sink, place a piece of cardboard over the top of the glass. Turn the glass upside down.

My Observations:

Why I think this happened: ______________________________

Experiment 2

Take a tea bag. Cut off the top and empty the tea leaves into the bin. Open the tea bag out so that it is long. Make sure that the tea bag is open along its length. Stand the tea bag on its end on the table. Light the top of the tea bag—the end away from the table.

My Observations:

Why I think this happened: ______________________________

Experiment 3

Place a candle in the center of a dish of water. (Make sure the candle is higher than the water.) Light the candle. Place a glass jar over the candle until it rests on the bottom of the dish.

My Observations:

Why I think this happened: ______________________________

Which experiment did you enjoy most? Find some other classmates who liked this experiment. Compare your reasons for the phenomena.

 © Teacher Created Materials, Inc.

Name:

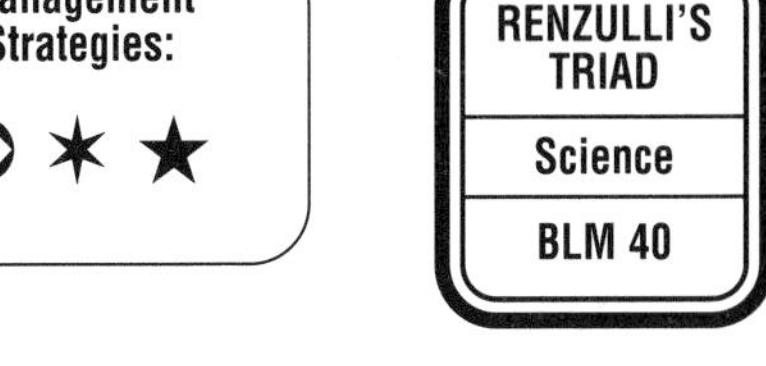

Type II—Research—Natural Disasters

1. From newspapers, magazines, etc., find pictures showing the following disasters and glue them on a separate sheet of paper.

Cyclone	Flood	Earthquake	Drought
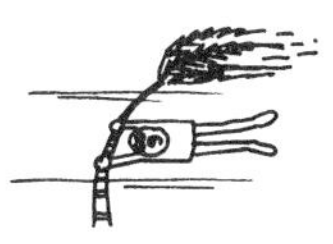			

2. Choose one of the disasters and find out the information to fill in the boxes below:

Type of Disaster:	
Causes (What causes it?)	
Effects (What are the effects of the disaster?)	
Prevention or safe guards (What can we do to prevent or lessen the effects?)	

3. Prepare a talk about this kind of disaster for your classmates. Use the information you have found and present your information in an interesting and different way.

Renzulli's Enrichment Triad for Social Studies

General

- Integrate SOSE across as many different subject areas as possible—language, math, art, science, technology, etc.
- Ensure learning and interest centers explore universal themes and values such as family, friendship, peace, cooperation, rules, cultural differences, acceptance, etc.
- Specific areas that can be studied or explored are anthropology, philosophy, genealogy, futurology, cartology, and market research strategies.
- Students need to be aware of and develop skills in all aspects of communication, for example, expressing points of view, arguing a case for or against, comparison, cause/effect, evaluating judgements, being objective or subjective, empathy and prejudice.

Type I

- Invite guests who can talk about change (over an extended period of time) in the community. Prior to their visit, ask students to prepare questions that will reveal whether the changes have been good or bad.
- Visit relevant places to observe how other societies and cultures differ from our own, for example, a museum, historical society village, consulate of another country, etc.
- Arrange for students to watch relevant documentaries to make comparisons about animal and human societies.
- Involve students in a brainstorm to identify cultures about which they would like to learn more. Group students so they can develop a web of related issues to pursue.

Type II

- Ask students to prepare and complete questionnaires, surveys, and interviews that require them to search for and state their values, attitudes, and beliefs on topics. For example:
  - Convicted criminals should not be allowed released early from jail.
  - People should be allowed to do what they want with the land they own.
- Engage students in discussions that involve moral and ethical issues. For example, discuss the actions of Goldilocks in the story of *The Three Bears*.
- Set up student research projects on early civilizations to explore their legacies.
- Organize student role-plays that relate to decision making. For example:
  - Conduct a trial of someone accused of being an arsonist and causing a bad forest fire.

Type III

- Allow students to complete investigations, either individually or as a small group, on topics of interest.
- Ask students to make out investigation plans detailing their goals, methods, time line, and information or knowledge they expect to learn from the investigations.
- Ask students to list all the different ways they can present their investigations to different audiences.

© Teacher Created Materials, Inc.

Name:

Type III—Investigation Plan

My topic is	
What I hope to find out (my goals):	
What I need to do to achieve my goals:	
What I need to know before I start:	
Who I will tell:	
How I will tell them:	
I will spend this much time on each part of my investigation:	Getting started _________ Achieving my goals _________ Preparing my presentation _________ Telling people about my investigation _________ Meeting with my mentor _________ (How often?) Other aspects _________

Evaluation of my investigation

Things I found useful:	Things I found that were not useful:
Things I did well:	Things that did not go very well:
I enjoyed this investigation because:	I did not enjoy this investigation because:

RENZULLI'S TRIAD
Creative Arts
ACTIVITIES

Renzulli's Enrichment Triad in Creative Arts

General

- Students should be able to experience all aspects of this curriculum during free time as well as during specific learning experiences.
- Include art and craft in all curriculum areas.
- Ensure that students experience all aspects of creative thinking such as fluency, flexibility, originality, elaboration, curiosity, complexity, risk-taking and imagination.
- Create interest/learning centers that explore areas such as: contemporary art, cartooning, the masters, different periods in art, puppetry, design of signs/houses/clothing, sculpture, pottery, etc.
- Display different types of art work around the room with technical and aesthetic information attached.

Type I

- Visit an art gallery.
- Organize an art workshop where different forms of art are taught by local artists or parents with an interest and expertise in these areas.
- Visit a graphic design studio or invite a graphic designer to talk to the students about their work.
- Make available paint, clay, craft material, etc. for students as media in which to express their ideas and feelings.

Type II

- Instigate research projects in which students study various artists employing a particular method in their work and then compare the work. For example:
  - Cubism as a form of expression.
  - Still lives that rely on texture or tone.
- Look at clothing design over the centuries. Ask students to take one particular item (dresses, pants, coats, swimming costumes) and chronicle the changes over time to this item. Students can design the item as it will look in another 50 years.
- Ask students to critique a piece of artwork—well known or one of their own.
- In small groups, ask students to plan an art exhibition. What types of art would they include? How would they present the art works?
- Look at sculpture and pottery from ancient civilizations and ask students to discuss their impact on society of today.

Type III

- Ask students to devise a plan for their investigation that includes preliminary sketches of any art work to be produced.
- Ask students to produce a piece of art work that they have developed using new or different techniques.
- Encourage students with a talent in a particular area of art/craft to hold an exhibition of their work, for their classmates or a larger audience.

 © Teacher Created Materials, Inc.

Name:

Management Strategies:

▼ ✶ ● ⊃

Type II—Ancient Civilizations

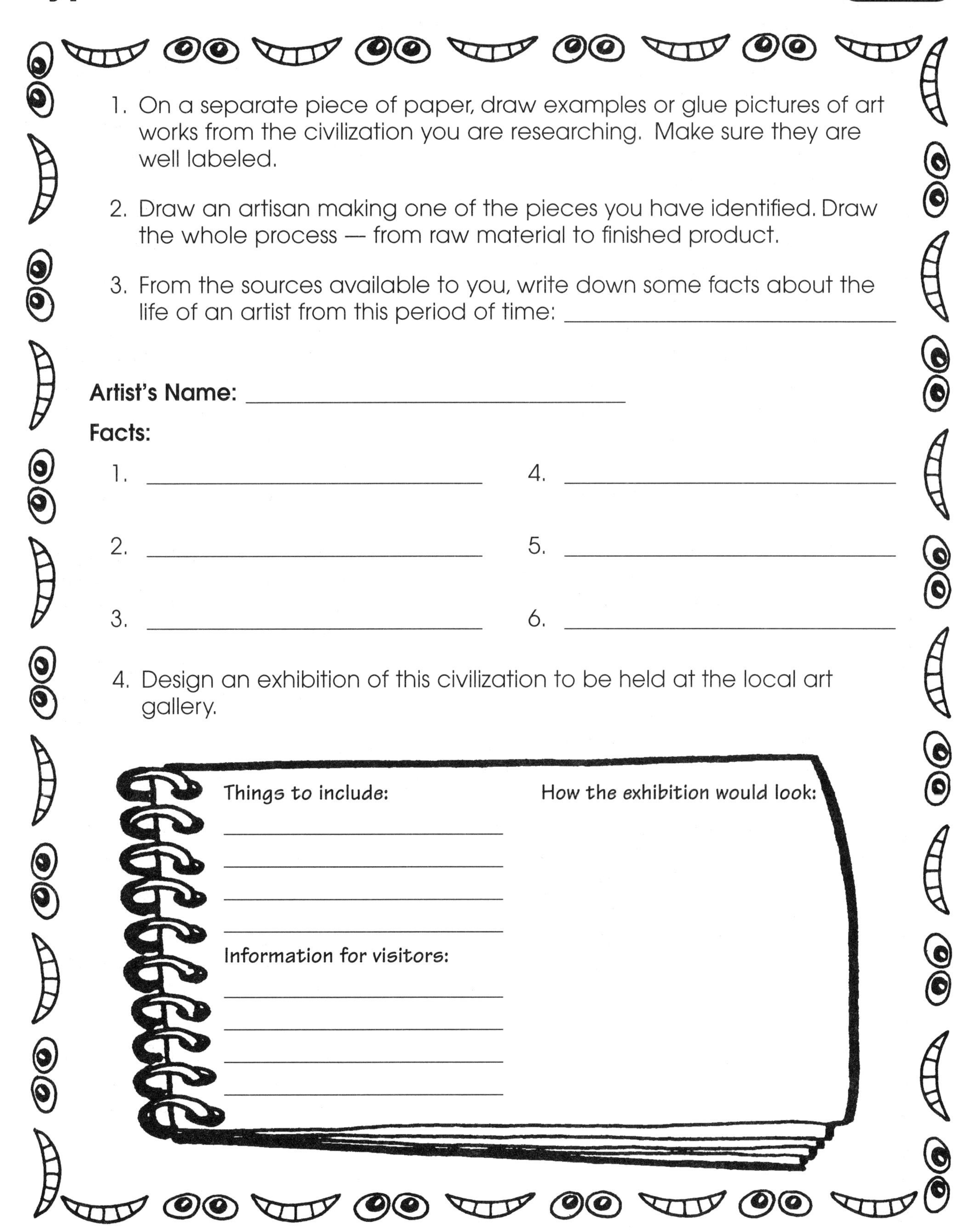

1. On a separate piece of paper, draw examples or glue pictures of art works from the civilization you are researching. Make sure they are well labeled.

2. Draw an artisan making one of the pieces you have identified. Draw the whole process — from raw material to finished product.

3. From the sources available to you, write down some facts about the life of an artist from this period of time: ______________________

Artist's Name: ______________________

Facts:

1. ______________________ 4. ______________________

2. ______________________ 5. ______________________

3. ______________________ 6. ______________________

4. Design an exhibition of this civilization to be held at the local art gallery.

Thinking Caps Notes and Activities

by Fay Holbert

 © Teacher Created Materials, Inc.

Overview for the Classroom Teacher

Introduction to Thinking Caps

The thinking caps are inspired by Dr. de Bono's concepts in teaching thinking skills. They provide a means whereby students can identify and utilize all their thinking processes when faced with an issue. They also help students to discuss their thinking processes.
Each cap represents a different thinking approach:

Cap	Uses	Purpose	Questions to Ask
Feelings Cap	• Making feelings known • Assessments and choices	• Alternatives • Emotions, feelings • Hunches, intuition	Which one do I like best? How do I feel about this?
Positive Cap	• Good points • Benefits • Why it will work • Likelihood	• Assessing and valuing • Extracting benefits • Making something work	Why is this worth doing? How will it help us? Why can it be done? Why will it help us?
Negative Cap	• Check for evidence • Check for logic • Feasibility • Impact • Weaknesses	• Find weaknesses • Makes assessments	Is this true? Will it work? What are the weaknesses? What is wrong with it?
Creative Cap	• Generate reactive ideas • Start ideas • Further, better, new ideas	• Creativity • Gives possibilities and alternatives	What are some ways to work this out /solve the problem? What ideas do we have?
Research Cap	• Identify what is relevant /most important/valid • Identify the information we have/need • Identify how to get the information we need	• Stimulate thinking • Check thinking	What information do we have? What information do we need to get?
Planning Cap	• Define focus/purpose • Set out thinking plan or agenda • Make observations and comments • Decide on the next step • Define outcomes • Summarize	• Be constructive • Thinking about thinking	What have we done so far? What do we do next? What is the next step? (often whole group)

* These students appear on the BLMs and task cards following to indicate some thinking strategies.

THINKING CAPS

NOTES

Overview for the Classroom Teacher

How Do the Caps Work?

The different caps allow students to approach an issue from six different points of view. Instead of trying to do everything at once, students learn to handle the different aspects of thinking one at a time. Finally, different aspects come together to give wide range thinking.

Our egos are very involved in our thinking. We get attached to an argument or an idea and find it difficult to stand back and be objective. The role playing in the thinking caps helps students to detach the ego from the thinking–"This is not me, but my positive cap speaking." With the thinking caps, if we don't like a suggestion, we know that there will always be a chance to criticize it with the negative cap and to express feelings with the feelings cap. Meanwhile, it is possible to explore the idea with the research, positive and creative caps.

It is very important that every thinker is able to switch roles: put caps on and take caps off. The purpose and value of the thinking caps is to get students to use all six modes of thinking.

Beware: We tend to overuse the negative cap. We tend to under-use the creative cap. When using the planning cap, be careful not to interrupt the line of thinking.

Four Styles for the Teacher to Use:

1. Put the cap on.

A child or a whole group:

"Give me some negative cap thinking."

"We're stuck. Can you put on your creative cap?"

2. Take the cap off.

Move away from a particular line of thinking:

"That's feeling cap thinking. Can you take off your feeling cap?"

"You've thought of lots of new ideas, but I think we should take off our creative caps now."

3. Switch caps.

This way we can call for a switch in thinking without hurting the student's feelings. We are not attacking the thinking, but asking for a change:

"We've heard the good things. Let's switch from the positive cap to the negative cap. What problems might there be if we do it like that?"

4. Signal your thinking.

Use the caps yourself and point out that you are using them as you teach the class.

Thinking Cap Sequences

The thinking caps are repeatedly used in sequence when we are confronted by more complicated thinking tasks. After a practice session, invite your students to recall the sequences they used. These observations provide a good basis for further discussions about the ways we approach thinking about problems and finding resolutions. Some common sequences are:

First Ideas: Planning – Research – Creative

Quick Assessment: Positive – Planning

Evaluation: Positive – Negative

Improvement: Negative – Creative

Explanation: Research – Creative

Direct Action: Feelings – Negative

Emotions: Feelings – Research – Creative – Planning

Caution: Research – Negative

Opportunity: Research – Positive

Design: Planning – Creative – Feelings

Possibilities: Creative – Planning

Useable Alternatives: Creative – Positive – Negative

Choice: Positive – Negative – Feelings

Final Assessment: Negative – Feelings

© Teacher Created Materials, Inc.

Thinking Caps for English

THINKING CAPS
English
Activities

Theme: Homes Around the World

Following are some thinking strategies on the theme of "Homes Around the World." . Ask students to approach each question wearing the caps nominated. For example, when discussing "What is a home?," ask students to put on their positive caps first and think of all the good things about what a home is and its benefits to people. Then ask them to change to their research caps and list all the information they can find about homes and houses. Finally, ask them to put on their feelings caps and discuss their feelings about homes.

Quick Assessment/First Ideas

- What are some synonyms for the words "house" and "home"? (Research)
- What is a home? Why do people need a home? (Positive, Research, Feelings)
- What was used to build your home? (Research)

Evaluation and Choice

- Are all homes the same?
  - Why?
  - Why not? (Research, Positive, Negative, Creative)
- What are some factors that influence the appearance and design of a house? (Planning, Positive, Negative, Feelings)

Assessment

- Can you tell by the appearance of a house which part of the world it comes from? (Planning, Positive, Feelings)
- Examine and then compare pictures and details of several houses (at least five).
  - Which one would be most suitable for your family? (Research, Planning, Positive, Negative, Feelings)
- In what ways is your home similar to, and different from, the homes of your friends? (Positive, Negative)

Caution

- Why wouldn't your present house be a possible choice in
  - Alaska?
  - the Sahara Desert?
  - the Sumatran Jungle? (Research, Negative, Feelings)

Wide-Range Thinking

- Ask students to collect pictures of houses from the real estate section of the local newspaper, including details of the buildings and the prices asked. Display these for all to examine.
  - What affects the prices of the houses?
  - Why do similar sized houses differ greatly in price? (All Caps)

THINKING CAPS
English
BLM 43

Name:

Homes Around the World

Management Strategies:

1. Why do Swiss chalets have sharply sloping roofs?

Why are Eskimos' igloos built from blocks of ice?

Why are many houses on the Carolina coast built high off the ground on tall piers?

Why are many homes on the Greek Islands painted white?

2. On another sheet of paper, draw an example of each of the four houses.

3. How many occupations might be involved in the construction of a house from the very beginning to the completed structure? Make a list of all occupations and the work each person would be responsible for performing.

Occupation	Work each person would do

© Teacher Created Materials, Inc.

Name:

Homes Around the World

1. People who live in some areas don't live in homes like yours. Complete this table showing the materials used in these traditional houses and why they are made this way.

Area	Made of:	Why?
Fiji (traditional)		
Alaska (Eskimo)		
Kenya (traditional)		
Malaysia (traditional)		
Remote farmland		

2. Where would I find the houses below? What are the differences between them and your home?

House	Where found?	What difference?	Why different?
Sampan			
Mia mia			
Teepee			
Caravan			
Whare			
Dacha			

3. Find some pictures of these houses, or illustrate them yourself.

   Choose one and make a 3-D model of the house, including labels to describe what it is made of, why it is made this way, and where it is found. (Use all caps.)

THINKING CAPS
English
TASK CARDS

Thinking Caps for English

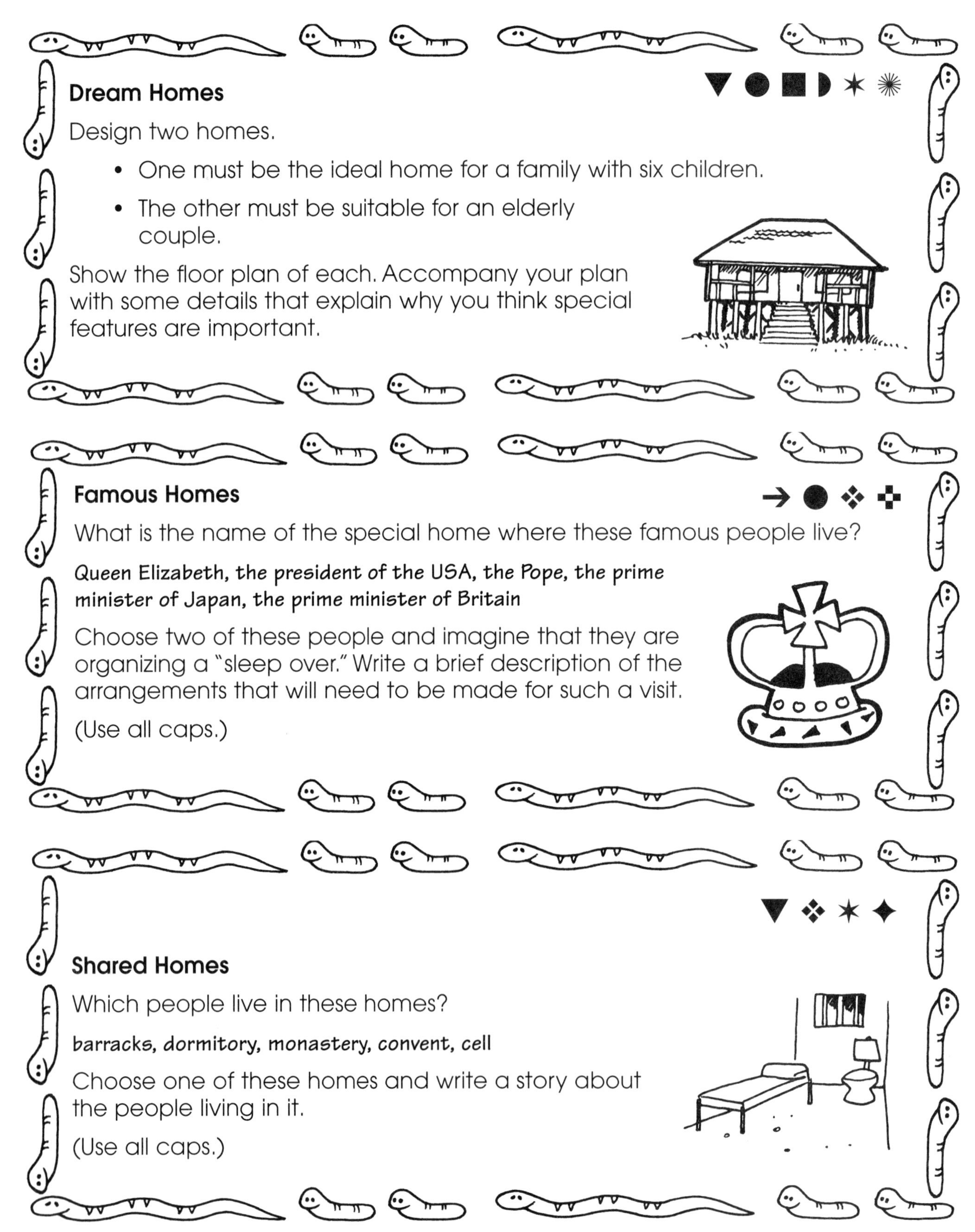

Dream Homes

Design two homes.

- One must be the ideal home for a family with six children.
- The other must be suitable for an elderly couple.

Show the floor plan of each. Accompany your plan with some details that explain why you think special features are important.

Famous Homes

What is the name of the special home where these famous people live?

Queen Elizabeth, the president of the USA, the Pope, the prime minister of Japan, the prime minister of Britain

Choose two of these people and imagine that they are organizing a "sleep over." Write a brief description of the arrangements that will need to be made for such a visit.

(Use all caps.)

Shared Homes

Which people live in these homes?

barracks, dormitory, monastery, convent, cell

Choose one of these homes and write a story about the people living in it.

(Use all caps.)

 © Teacher Created Materials, Inc.

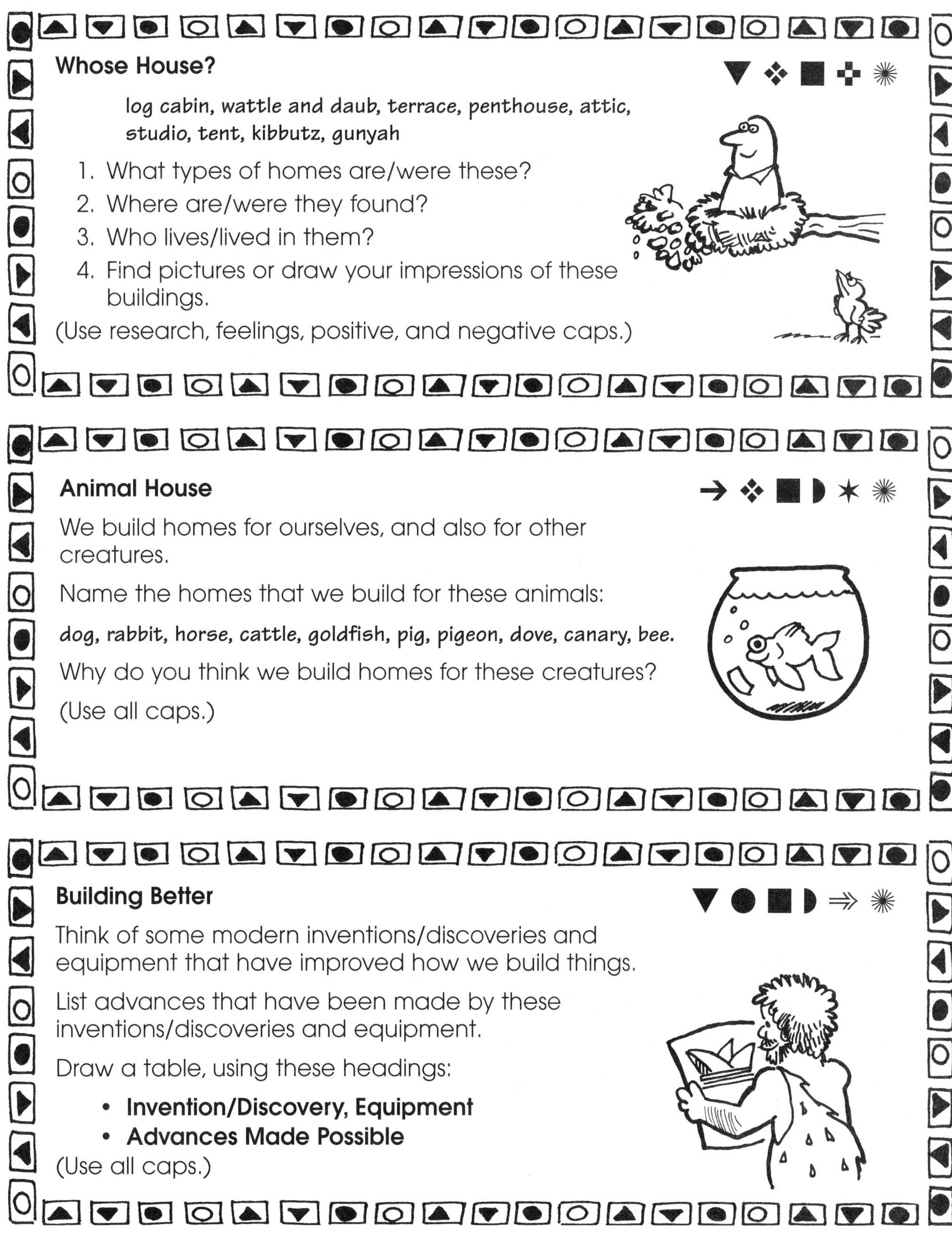

Whose House?

▼ ❖ ■ ✜ ✳

log cabin, wattle and daub, terrace, penthouse, attic, studio, tent, kibbutz, gunyah

1. What types of homes are/were these?
2. Where are/were they found?
3. Who lives/lived in them?
4. Find pictures or draw your impressions of these buildings.

(Use research, feelings, positive, and negative caps.)

Animal House

→ ❖ ■ ◗ ★ ✳

We build homes for ourselves, and also for other creatures.

Name the homes that we build for these animals:

dog, rabbit, horse, cattle, goldfish, pig, pigeon, dove, canary, bee.

Why do you think we build homes for these creatures?

(Use all caps.)

Building Better

▼ ● ■ ◗ ⇒ ✳

Think of some modern inventions/discoveries and equipment that have improved how we build things.

List advances that have been made by these inventions/discoveries and equipment.

Draw a table, using these headings:

- **Invention/Discovery, Equipment**
- **Advances Made Possible**

(Use all caps.)

THINKING CAPS
Math
ACTIVITIES

Thinking Caps for Math

Theme: Measurement—Informal Units

Begin by asking students to identify the standard measurements they are familiar with. Then move the discussion to look at other ways of measuring and the consequences of working with informal units.

Sharing Information

- What instruments/tools do we use to measure length? Name the most commonly used length measurements. (Research)
- What instruments/tools do we use to measure weight? Name the most commonly used weight measurements. (Research)
- What instruments/tools do we use to measure capacity? Name the most commonly used capacity measurements. (Research)

Possibilities and Alternatives

- If we had no standardized measurements what could we use to measure
  - length?
  - weight?
  - capacity? (Creative, Positive, Planning)

Possibilities, Design, and Explanation

- If you and two friends were asked to measure the length of your desk with your own pencil, what could be some of the problems you would encounter in stating the result in "pencils"? (Planning, Creative, Research, Feelings)
- What could you use to determine equal weights when you have no scales? (Creative)
- If you wanted to buy some fruit and there were no scales in the shop, how could you be told prices? Would this be a fair way to buy and sell? (Creative, Negative, Positive, Feelings)
- How could you estimate the height of a person when you cannot use standard units—meters and centimeters? (Planning, Creative)

Assessment

- How difficult would it be to write out a recipe if you could not show quantities in grams of ingredients such as flour and sugar? (Planning, Positive, Feelings)

Wide-Range Thinking

- If standard weights were not available, suggest some informal units that could be used to indicate the following:
  - length
  - weight
  - capacity

  Would this always be fair for both the buyer and the seller? (All Caps)

 © Teacher Created Materials, Inc.

Name:

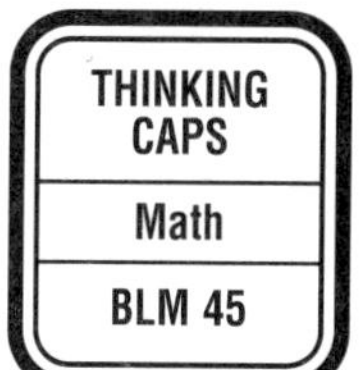

Informal Units

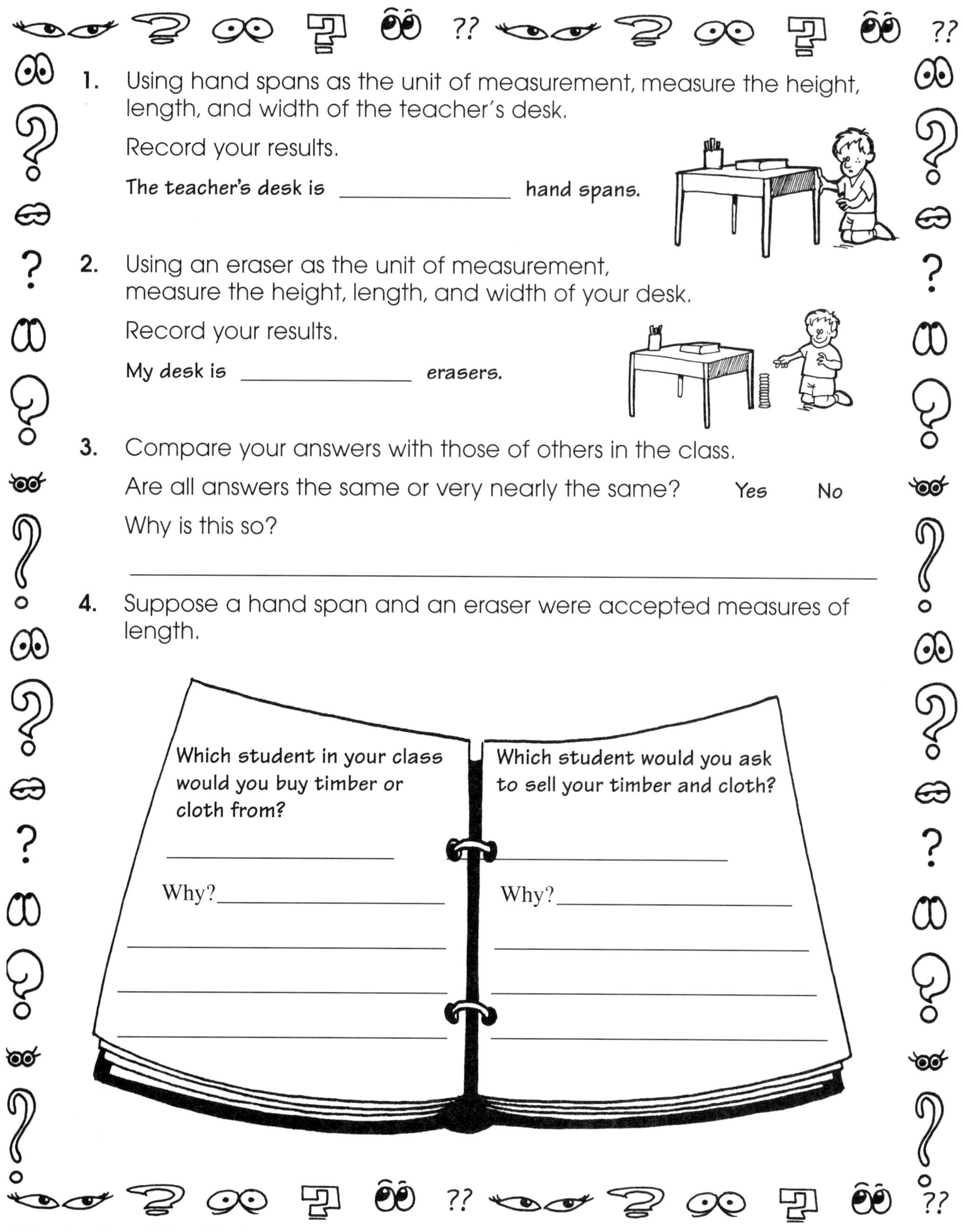

1. Using hand spans as the unit of measurement, measure the height, length, and width of the teacher's desk.

   Record your results.

   The teacher's desk is ______________ hand spans.

2. Using an eraser as the unit of measurement, measure the height, length, and width of your desk.

   Record your results.

   My desk is ______________ erasers.

3. Compare your answers with those of others in the class.

   Are all answers the same or very nearly the same? Yes No

   Why is this so?

   ____

4. Suppose a hand span and an eraser were accepted measures of length.

THINKING CAPS

Math

BLM 46

Name:

Management Strategies:

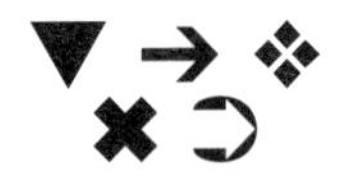

Measurement Mysteries

1. Find three other friends and solve these mysteries:

   Fred sells flour and potatoes in the market. In this market, a bucket filled with sand – a "sacket" – is the accepted measure of weight. Fred is a dishonest seller. He makes a huge profit selling his flour at an advertised price of $3 per sacket. How does he do this?

   Frieda is a sly buyer at Fred's stall. She needs a sacket of potatoes. Somehow she always seems to get more for her sacket than other more honest buyers. How does she do this?

2. In your group, develop a short sketch that illustrates the use of sackets and hand spans by both a buyer and a seller in a marketplace, both of whom are only interested in making/saving money.

 © Teacher Created Materials, Inc.

Name:

Management Strategies:

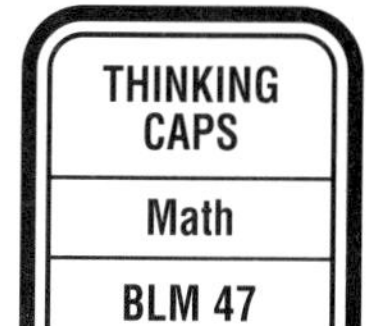

Comparison

1. Form a group of three. Come up with several different units that could be used to measure the subjects listed:

Subject	Informal Measuring Units	Advantages	Disadvantages
Height of a friend			
Height of a teacher			
Height of a chair			
Width of classroom			
Height of a fence			
Length of a car			
Height of the board			

2. In groups of three, measure three of the subjects above, using three different informal units.

Subject 1:		Subject 2:		Subject 3:	
Unit 1:	Result:	Unit 1:	Result:	Unit 1:	Result:
Unit 2:	Result:	Unit 2:	Result:	Unit 2:	Result:
Unit 3:	Result:	Unit 3:	Result:	Unit 3:	Result:

THINKING CAPS
Math
TASK CARDS

Thinking Caps for Math

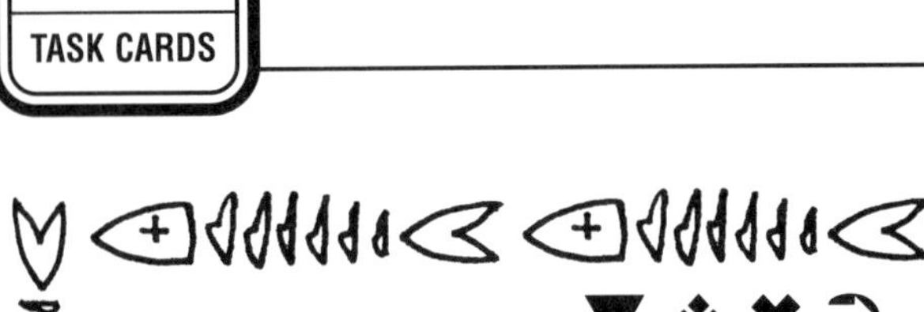

Spoonfuls of Measurement

Find three friends and bring a variety of spoons to school—as many sizes as possible.

Which friend would you ask to give you a spoonful of chocolate or something you really like? Why?

Which student would you ask to give you a spoonful of medicine or something that has a dreadful taste? Why?

Maintaining Standards

Write down your responses to these questions:

1. Can you see a need for standardized weights and measures?
2. Why do you think this way?
3. Who would be responsible for standardizing all weights and measures?
4. Explain your choice.

(Use all caps.)

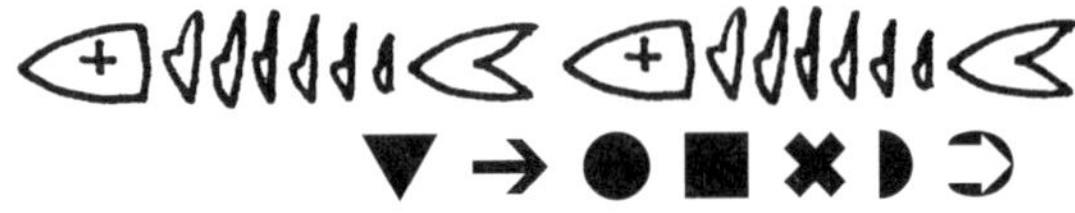

Rubbery Robbery

Imagine you are a witness to a robbery.

Give your description of the criminal to the police officer, using informal units of measurement: height, weight, size of the loot bag, the getaway car, etc.

Draw your robber for further identification.

What are some of the problems with this method of description?

(Use all caps.)

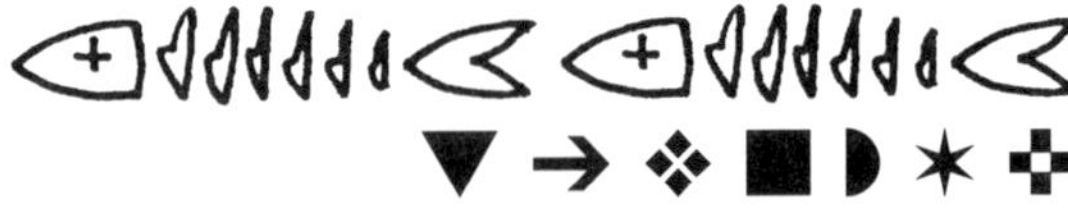

Global Measurement

Find out which countries have the same system of measurement as ours and which do not.

What would happen if only some countries accepted standardized measures while others remained with informal units?

List all your ideas.

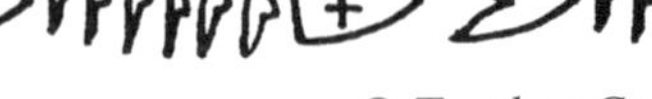

 © Teacher Created Materials, Inc.

Thinking Caps for Health

THINKING CAPS
Health
ACTIVITIES

Theme: Keeping Healthy

Begin the discussion by clarifying what "health" means and what contributes to good health. Ask students to consider their experiences of the health system through vaccinations, visits to the dentist, and hospital visits. Ask them to look at their growth and development and the kinds of sports they are involved in. Finally, revisit what it means to be healthy.

First Thoughts

- What does being healthy mean? (Research, Planning, Feelings)
- How does food make a difference to our health? (Research, Positive, Negative, Feelings)
  - How many pieces of fruit do you eat each day? (Research)
  - How many servings of vegetables do you have each day? (Research)
- What else contributes to good health? (Planning, Research, Creative)

Sharing Experiences/Information

- Have you had all of your vaccinations against diseases such as diphtheria, whooping cough, tetanus, polio, rubella, etc.? Can you remember when you had the vaccinations? (Research, Positive, Feelings)
- When was the last time you visited a dentist? (Research)
- When is your next dental appointment? (Research)
- How many fillings and/or extractions of your second teeth have you had? (Planning Research)
- Have you ever been admitted to a hospital due to illness or an accident?
  - What was wrong?
  - What did your doctor advise you to do to recover? (Research, Planning, Positive, Negative)

Personal Statistics

- Let's talk about how you're growing:
  - How tall are you?
  - How much do you weigh?
  - Are you happy with your build? Why/Why not? (Positive, Negative, Feelings)
- Let's talk about how fit you are.
  - How long does it take you to walk briskly around the school?
  - Can you jog around the school without being puffed out?
  - Time yourself on both of these activities. (Research, Positive, Negative, Feelings)
  - In which sporting teams do you represent your school? Which community sports do you participate in? Do you enjoy this time? (Research, Feelings)
- Do you play games like chess, dominoes, checkers or have hobbies like art, music, drama, etc.? Do you enjoy this time too? (Research, Feelings)

What Does It Mean to Be Healthy?

- How much time do you spend talking with your parents and brothers and sisters about normal everyday things that happen to you? (Planning, Positive, Feelings)
- Why is it important to be healthy mentally and emotionally as well as physically? (All Caps)

THINKING CAPS
Health
BLM 48

Name:

Food and Exercise Diary

1. Keep a daily record of what you eat for one week. Complete this table about foods you like to eat:

Foods I should eat and drink often:	Foods I shouldn't eat and drink often:

2. Compare how much time you spend sitting down with how much time you spend doing physical activities. The table below will help you:

Sitting Activities	Mon	Tues	Wed	Thurs	Fri	Sat	Sun
Reading							
Watching TV							
Studying							
Homework							
At school							
Physical Activities							
Games							
Sport							
Walking							
Shopping							

3. What are some simple activities you can do at home or with your family and at school to help improve your fitness and health? Illustrate your ideas.

© Teacher Created Materials, Inc.

Thinking Caps for Health

THINKING CAPS
Health
TASK CARDS

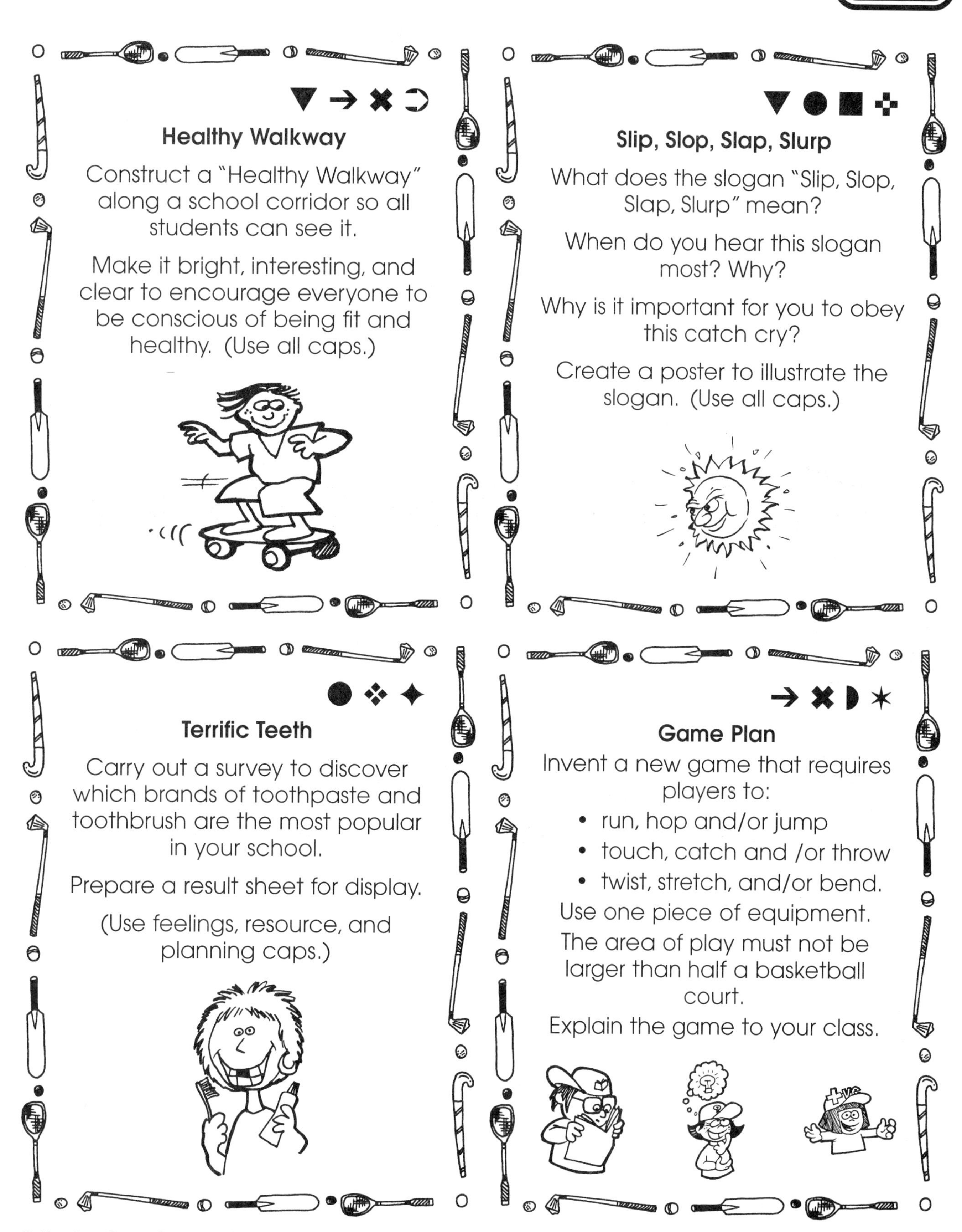

Healthy Walkway

Construct a "Healthy Walkway" along a school corridor so all students can see it.

Make it bright, interesting, and clear to encourage everyone to be conscious of being fit and healthy. (Use all caps.)

Slip, Slop, Slap, Slurp

What does the slogan "Slip, Slop, Slap, Slurp" mean?

When do you hear this slogan most? Why?

Why is it important for you to obey this catch cry?

Create a poster to illustrate the slogan. (Use all caps.)

Terrific Teeth

Carry out a survey to discover which brands of toothpaste and toothbrush are the most popular in your school.

Prepare a result sheet for display.

(Use feelings, resource, and planning caps.)

Game Plan

Invent a new game that requires players to:

- run, hop and/or jump
- touch, catch and /or throw
- twist, stretch, and/or bend.

Use one piece of equipment.

The area of play must not be larger than half a basketball court.

Explain the game to your class.

THINKING CAPS
Creative Arts
ACTIVITIES

Thinking Caps for Creative Arts

Theme: Patterns and Designs

The following notes provide some strategies for students to explore patterns and tessellation. The theme is continued by looking at other forms of structured pattern making — tapestry and silk-screen printing. Finally, it is taken out into the practical everyday world of signs — their functions and design.

Tessellation—First Thoughts

- Provide pictures of some designs, patterns and tessellations from books, magazines, newspapers and brochures.
- Ask students about patterns and the terminology used:
  - What are patterns and designs?
  - What is a 'tessellation'? (Research)
  - Where have you seen tessellations? (Research, Planning)
- Locate some patterns and designs in your classroom. (Research)

Tessellation - Research and Exploration

- Visit a tile or brick showroom. Examine some of the display work.
  - Which displays do you like best/least?
  - Why? (Feelings, Positive, Negative)
- Speak with some of the employees there.
  - How is the work done?
  - Why is this type of work needed? (Planning, Research)
- Ask students:
  - How they might apply this work to their room or home. (Research, Planning, Creative)
  - What shapes are commonly used? Why? (Planning, Creative, Research)

Tapestry and Silk Screen Printing—Research and Exploration

- Visit a craft shop, or invite a craft shop manager to come to your class to speak about tapestries, show what this kind of work looks like, and how to do it. Ask students to prepare questions:
  - What equipment is needed?
  - When was tapestry work first done?
  - Where?
  - Why? (All Caps)
- Invite creative arts teachers and students from TAFE and the high school to come to your school and show you how to do this craft. (Creative, Research, Planning, Positive)
  - What is "silk-screen printing"?

Signs—First Thoughts

- Brainstorm:
  - What are some common signs (containing no words) that you see every day?
  - Why do we use signs? (Positive, Creative, Negative)
  - Who do signs benefit most? (Planning, Research, Feelings)

Signs-Wide-Range Thinking

- Ask students to identify the important features about a successful sign? (All Caps)
- Take students on a short walk around your school or local community. Ask students:
  - What signs do you see?
  - Do you understand what they mean?
  - Why are they in that place? (All Caps)
  - What attracts your attention to these signs? (All Caps)

 © Teacher Created Materials, Inc.

Name:

Tessellations

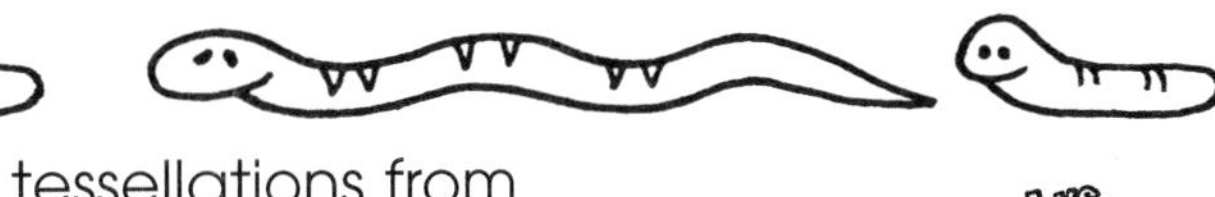

1. Collect colored pictures of six tessellations from magazines or brochures and paste them onto a large sheet of paper.

2. Draw and name the shapes that have been used in each tessellation.

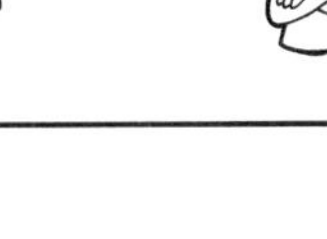

3. **Copy one of your examples here and color it identically to the picture.**	
4. **Now in this space, use the same colors but in a different way. Which one do you like better?**	

5. Use cardboard for this project.
   - Cut out several of your own shaped pieces—include triangles, squares, rectangles and hexagons.
   - Paint them your chosen colors.
   - Use them to create your own tessellation.

Plan your design here:

THINKING CAPS
Creative Arts
TASK CARDS

Thinking Caps for Creative Arts

Tapestry

On a sheet of graph paper, 12 inches square, create your own tapestry design with a specific theme, showing all colors to be used.

Transfer your design onto special tapestry cloth and work the tapestry.

(Use all caps.)

Silk Screen Prints

Prepare a silk-screen design that is suitable for a T-shirt, for

- your school
- your sporting team
- another group you belong to

Consider the colors you will use, size of the design and the color of the T-shirt to be printed.

(Use all caps.)

Signs and Logos

What are some of the most common signs/logos that you see every day in your community?

Illustrate your favorite ones.

Remember that correct color is often a most important part of the plan.

(Use research, feelings, positive, and planning caps.)

De-sign

Design a sign for a place you consider needs to be made more obvious to the people of your community.

(Use all caps.)

Make Your Own Task Cards

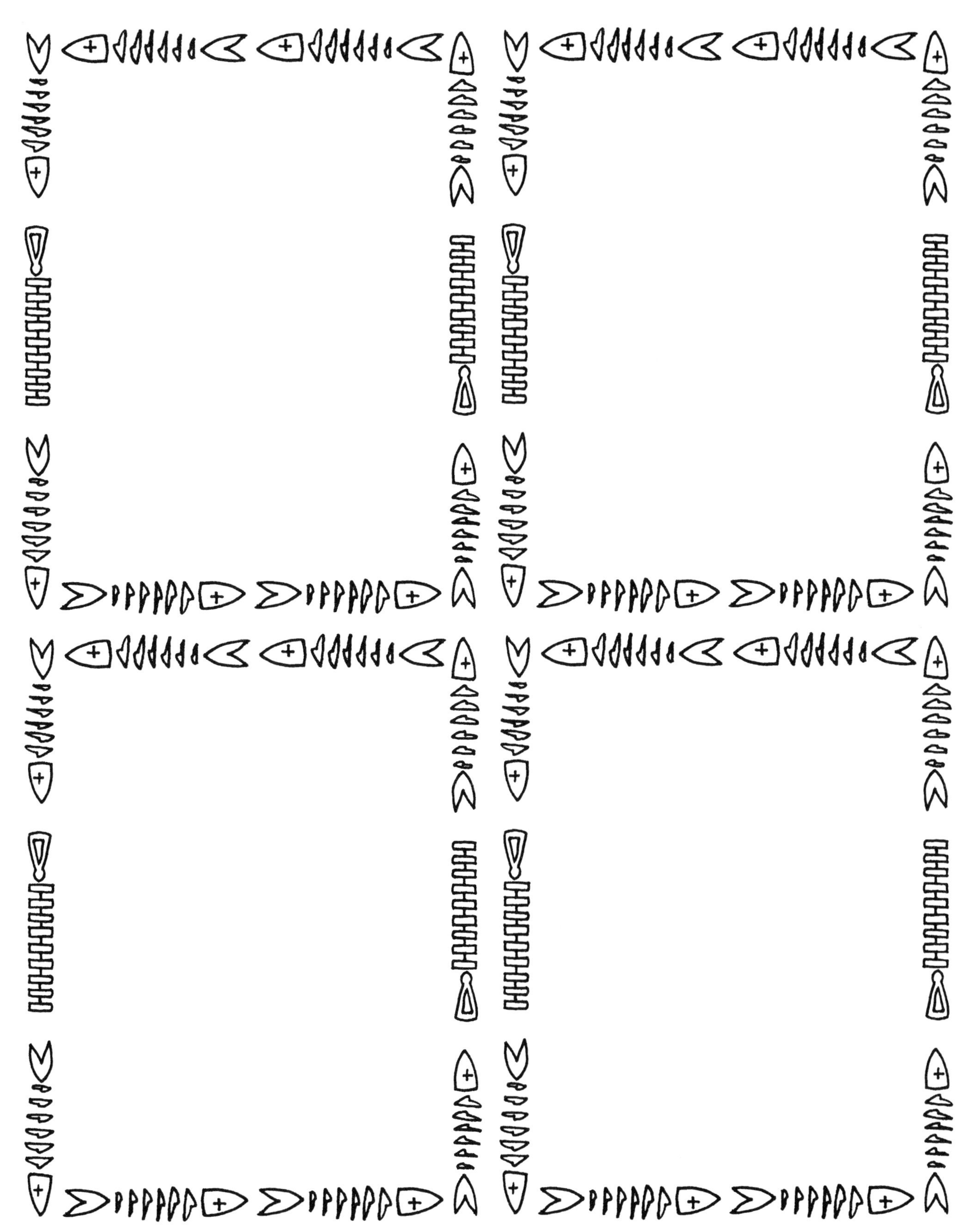

Gardner's Multiple Intelligences Notes and Activities

by Fay Holbert

 © Teacher Created Materials, Inc.

Overview for the Classroom Teacher

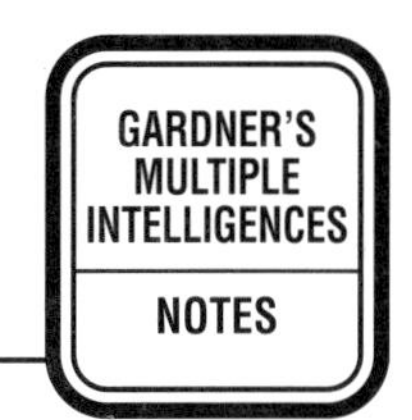

Introduction to Howard Gardner's Multiple Intelligences

Gardner defines intelligence as the ability to solve problems, or to create products, that are valued within one or more cultural setting/s. He maintains that it should be possible to identify an individual's educational profile at an early age and then draw upon this knowledge to enhance that person's educational opportunities and options. An educator should be able to channel individuals with unusual talents into special enrichment programs. To this end, he has developed a framework, building on the theory of multiple intelligences, that can be applied to any educational situation.

Because of Gardner's work, many educators believe that education is not merely a means to sort out a few children and make them leaders but to develop the latent talents of the entire population in diverse ways.

If we are to understand our children's potential, we must take into consideration all of their abilities and not just those that can be tested with standardized instruments such as an I.Q. test. What is important in educational terms is not which intelligences we are strongest in but our own particular blend of strengths and weaknesses.

The importance attached to the I.Q., however, is not entirely inappropriate the score does predict a person's ability to achieve in school subjects. Its limitation is that it predicts little of the successes in later life.

So, what of the wider range of performances that are valued in different parts of the world? For example, a 12-year-old boy from the Caroline Islands who has shown some ability is selected by his elders to learn how to become a master sailor and undertake study of navigation, geography, and the stars; and a 15-year-old Iranian youth who has committed to heart the entire Koran and mastered the Arabic language will train to be a teacher and religious leader.

It is obvious that these two young people are displaying intelligent behavior, and it is equally clear that the present method of assessing intellect is not going to allow an accurate assessment of their potential or their achievements. Only if we expand and rethink our views of what counts as human intellect will we, as educators, be able to devise more appropriate ways of assessing it and more effective ways of educating it.

Gardner's "Intelligences":

- Verbal/Linguistic
- Logical/Mathematical
- Visual/Spatial
- Bodily/Kinesthetic
- Musical/Rhythmical
- Interpersonal
- Intrapersonal

Recently Gardner has added a new intelligence: Nature/Environmental.

Learning Centers

The classroom teacher should give equal time and attention to each intelligence every day. One way to achieve this is to maintain various learning centers in the classroom.

- The Shakespeare Center **(Verbal/ Linguistic)**
- The Einstein Center **(Logical/ Mathematical)**
- The da Vinci Center **(Visual/Spatial)**
- The Edison Center **(Bodily/Kinesthetic)**
- The Fitzgerald Center **(Musical/Rhythmical)**
- The Chisholm Center **(Interpersonal)**
- The Keller Center **(Intrapersonal)**
- The Leakey Center **(Nature/ Environmental)**

A Note About This Section

This section looks at one theme from the perspective of the various intelligences.

Overview for the Classroom Teacher

Details and Description of Gardner's Multiple Intelligences

Verbal/Linguistic (V/L)

This student enjoys words—reading, writing, storytelling, humor/jokes. He/she participates eagerly in debates, story/poetry writing, journal/diary keeping and has a sensitivity to language.

- *writer, poet, novelist, journalist, psycho-linguist (L/M), signing*

Logical/Mathematical (L/M)

This student loves numbers, patterns, relationships, formulas. He/she shines at mathematics, reasoning, logic, problem solving, and deciphering codes and enjoys pattern games, calculation, number sequences, outlining.

- *scientist, mathematician, engineer, technician*

Visual/Spatial (V/S)

This student loves drawing, building, designing, creating, visualizing colors, pictures, observing, patterns/designs. He/she enjoys creating models, mind mapping, pretending and has an active imagination.

- *artist, cartographer, navigator, decorator, chess player*

Bodily/Kinesthetic (B/K)

This student has to touch, move, handle objects. He/she enjoys dance, drama, role-play, mime, sports games, physical gestures, martial arts and is great with body control, refining movement, expression through movement, inventing, interaction.

- *athlete, surgeon (L/M), dancer/choreographer (M/R)*

Musical/Rhythmical (M/R)

This student loves sounds, melody, rhythm, playing instruments, singing, vocal sounds/tones. He/she needs to be involved with music composition/creation, and music performances and enjoys percussion, humming, environmental/instrumental sounds, tonal and rhythmic patterns.

- *musician, composer, sound engineer (L/M), music critic (V/L)*

Interpersonal (Ier)

The student who likes interacting, talking, giving and receiving feedback, group projects, cooperative learning strategies, division of labor. He/she needs to be involved in collaborative tasks and person-to-person communication. This student is always intuitive about others' feelings and motives and is empathetic.

- *administrator, coach, mental health, physician (L/M), teacher (various)*

Intrapersonal (Ira)

This student wants to work alone, pursue personal interests, understands self, and has introspective feelings and dreams. He/she displays silent reflective methods, higher order reasoning and metacognition techniques, emotional processing, focus/concentration skills, complex guided imagery, centering practices.

- *writer (V/L), inventor (L/M)*

Nature/Environmental (N/E)

Recently, Gardner has included an eighth intelligence which he calls "Nature/Environmental." Not a lot of information is yet available from Gardner on this intelligence, but it is summarized as one involving the recognition and classification of species in the environment and how we can best preserve this environment for the greatest benefit to all.

- *veterinarian, zoologist, botanist, national park ranger, landscape gardener (V/L), florist*

Note: The "students" described here appear on the task cards and BLMs that follow to indicate the "intelligence" to which that activity is primarily targeted.

© Teacher Created Materials, Inc.

Gardner's Multiple Intelligences Activities

Theme: Communication

Many of the activities that follow are not exclusive to one intelligence but may involve two or more. For example, those asking for illustrations involve Visual/Spatial and those requiring oral and/or written presentations involve Verbal/Linguistic, etc.

Where questions could be answered with a "yes" or "no" response, probe for more information.

Verbal/Linguistic

- What does "communication" mean?
- To communicate, both the sender and the receiver must understand the method of the message. Why?
- If you speak only English, can you communicate orally with someone who speaks only Japanese?
- Name some methods of communication that you regularly use.
- Who would be different? Why?

Logical/Mathematical

- What are codes? Who uses them?
- Why do these people need to use codes?
- Name some codes that are often used.
- What are hieroglyphs and cuneiform?
- Why do experts have such difficulty understanding these?

Visual/Spatial

- Name some signs that we frequently see.
- Why do we use these signs?
- If there were no signs allowed, list some alternatives. Would these alternatives be successful? Why?
- How can a message be communicated without speech or writing?
- What other means of communication were used by early civilizations?
- Can art be a means of communication?

Bodily/Kinesthetic

- Send a message to the class, using only mime or movement.
- Express feelings – but use no words.
- What is "Auslan"? Who uses it? Why?
- How does dance communicate?
- When music is played over a public address system, how do people react?
- How do most people react at a concert? Why?

Musical/Rhythmical

- How can you communicate using only music?
- When you watch a movie, what is the effect of the music?
- How do composers create the mood of sad, haunting, or tired/exhausted music?
  - Which instruments are often used to communicate these emotions?
- Express emotions without using words. What other emotions can you communicate through sounds?

Interpersonal

- Which people cannot take advantage of modern communications?
- Why do some students in your class/school have difficulty with reading, writing and/or speaking English? Describe these difficulties. How can you help?

Intrapersonal

- List some of the difficulties for a student when learning to read and write if he or she is hearing or visually impaired.
- Wear a blindfold or earplugs and try to participate in a lesson for a few minutes.
  - What sensations do you experience?
  - What could others do for you?

Nature/Environmental

- What signs of communication networks do you see in your community? Do you think these spoil your environment? Explain. What can be done about them?
- List community concerns about modern communications.

GARDNER'S MULTIPLE INTELLIGENCES

BLM 50

Name:

Ways of Communicating

Management Strategies:

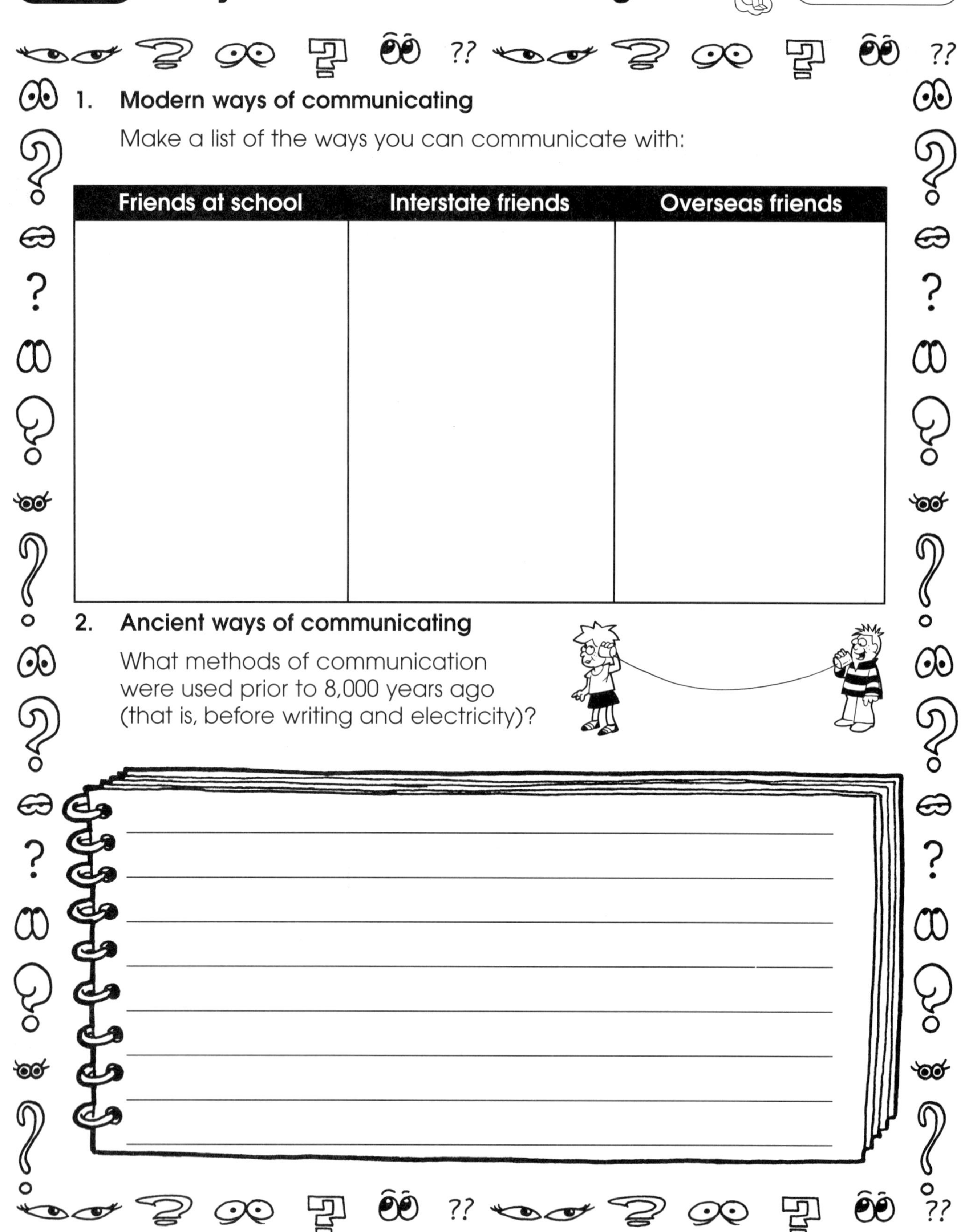

1. **Modern ways of communicating**

   Make a list of the ways you can communicate with:

Friends at school	Interstate friends	Overseas friends

2. **Ancient ways of communicating**

   What methods of communication were used prior to 8,000 years ago (that is, before writing and electricity)?

© Teacher Created Materials, Inc.

Activities for Communication

Signs

Illustrate signs that are displayed in the community:

- on and beside roads
- around shopping centers
- in playgrounds

Explain to your class what each one means.

Alphabets

1. On the map below, name and mark the countries where these alphabets are used:

   Cyrillic   Arabic   Hebrew   Sanskrit

2. Find out how long each alphabet has been used.

GARDNER'S MULTIPLE INTELLIGENCES

BLM 51

Name:

Management Strategies:

Imagine

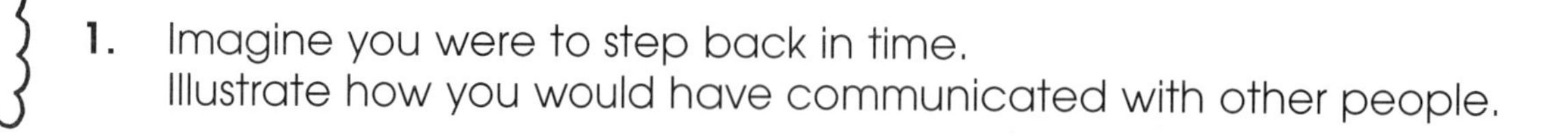

1. Imagine you were to step back in time.
   Illustrate how you would have communicated with other people.

5,000 years ago	1,000 years ago	100 years ago

2. Now imagine you step forward in time.
   Illustrate what you think you will be using to communicate with people in another city 100 years from now. Write a description and draw a picture in the notebook below.

© Teacher Created Materials, Inc.

Activities for Communication

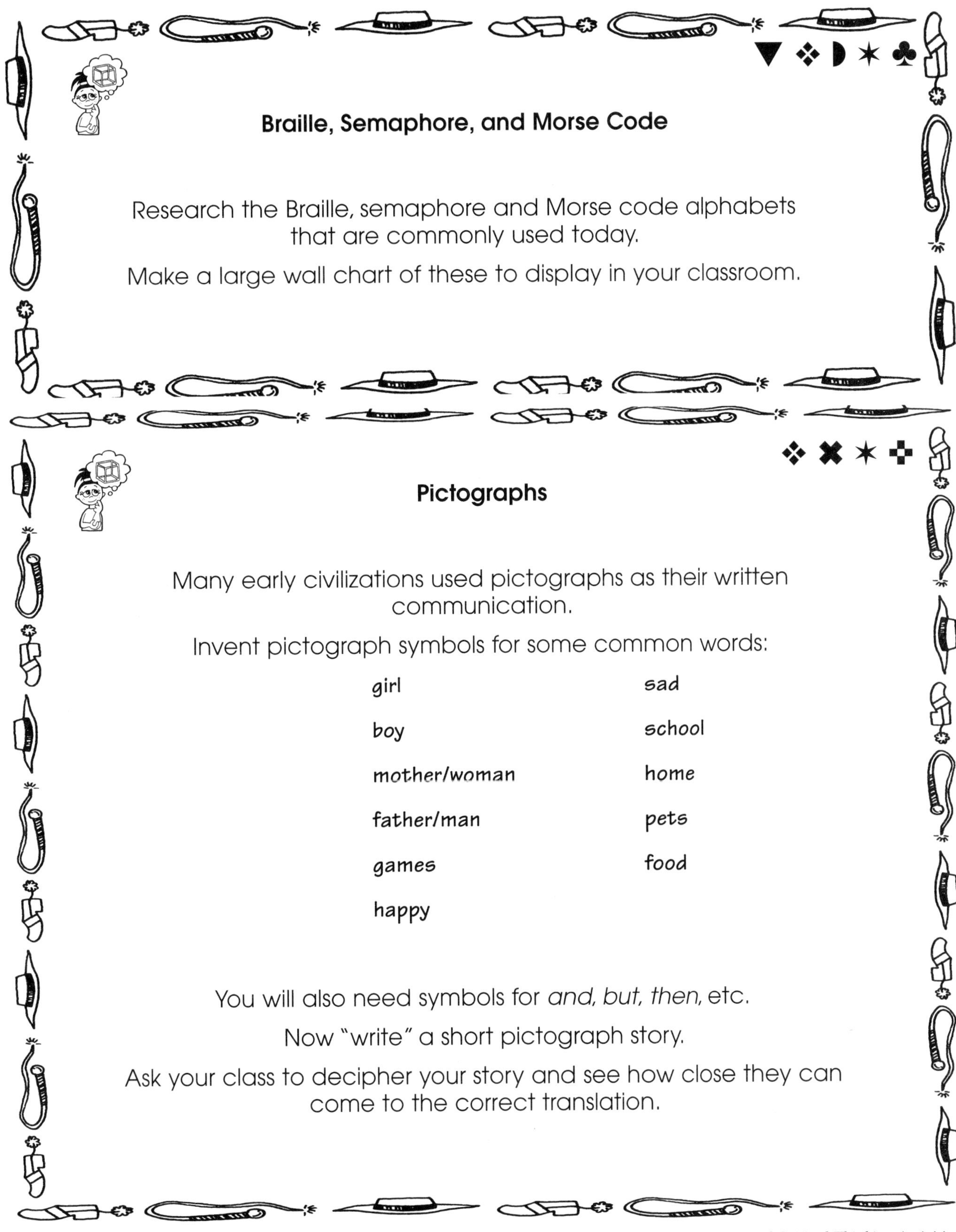

Braille, Semaphore, and Morse Code

Research the Braille, semaphore and Morse code alphabets that are commonly used today.

Make a large wall chart of these to display in your classroom.

Pictographs

Many early civilizations used pictographs as their written communication.

Invent pictograph symbols for some common words:

girl	sad
boy	school
mother/woman	home
father/man	pets
games	food
happy	

You will also need symbols for *and, but, then,* etc.

Now "write" a short pictograph story.

Ask your class to decipher your story and see how close they can come to the correct translation.

Activities for Communication

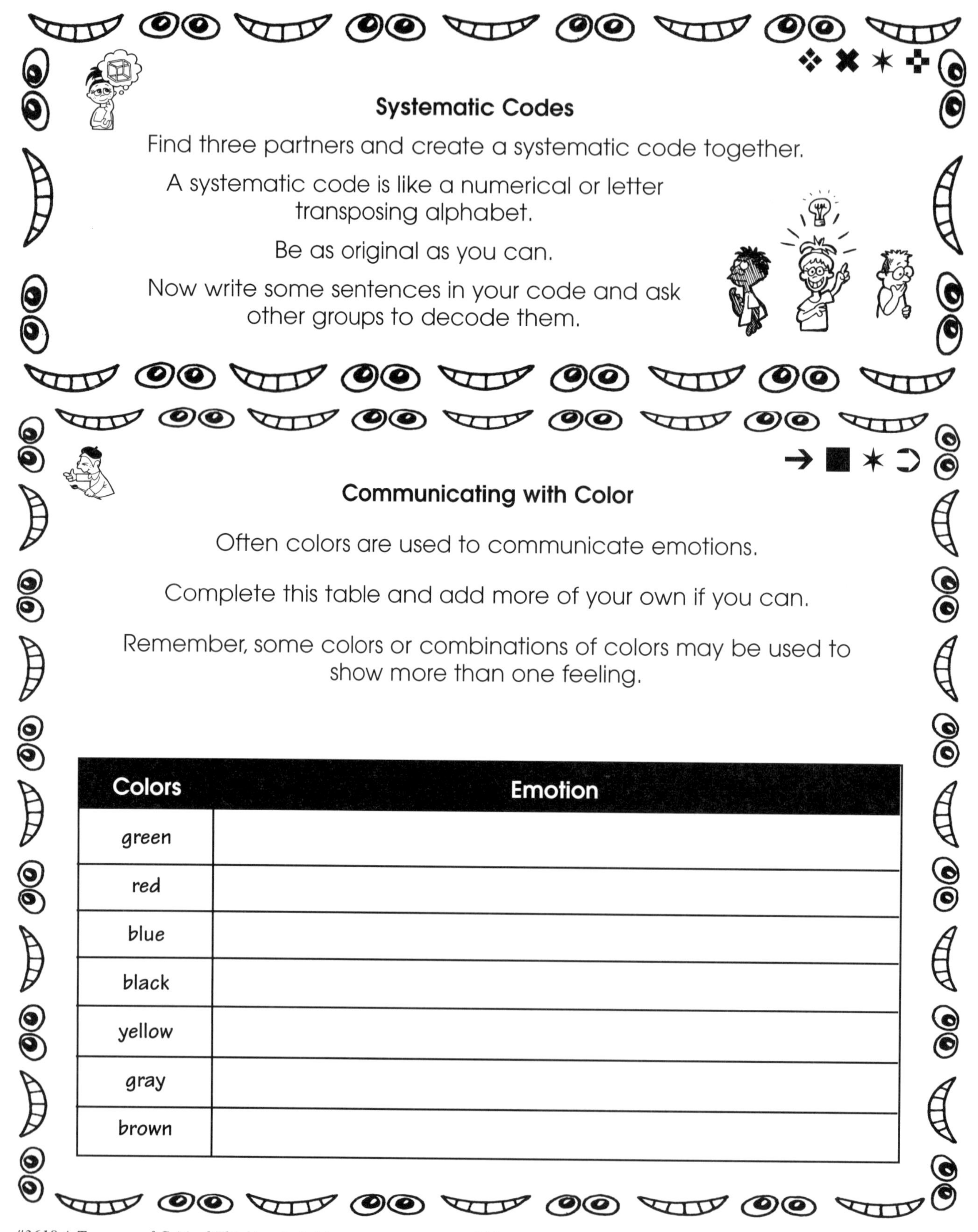

Systematic Codes

Find three partners and create a systematic code together.

A systematic code is like a numerical or letter transposing alphabet.

Be as original as you can.

Now write some sentences in your code and ask other groups to decode them.

Communicating with Color

Often colors are used to communicate emotions.

Complete this table and add more of your own if you can.

Remember, some colors or combinations of colors may be used to show more than one feeling.

Colors	Emotion
green	
red	
blue	
black	
yellow	
gray	
brown	

 © Teacher Created Materials, Inc.

Activities for Communication

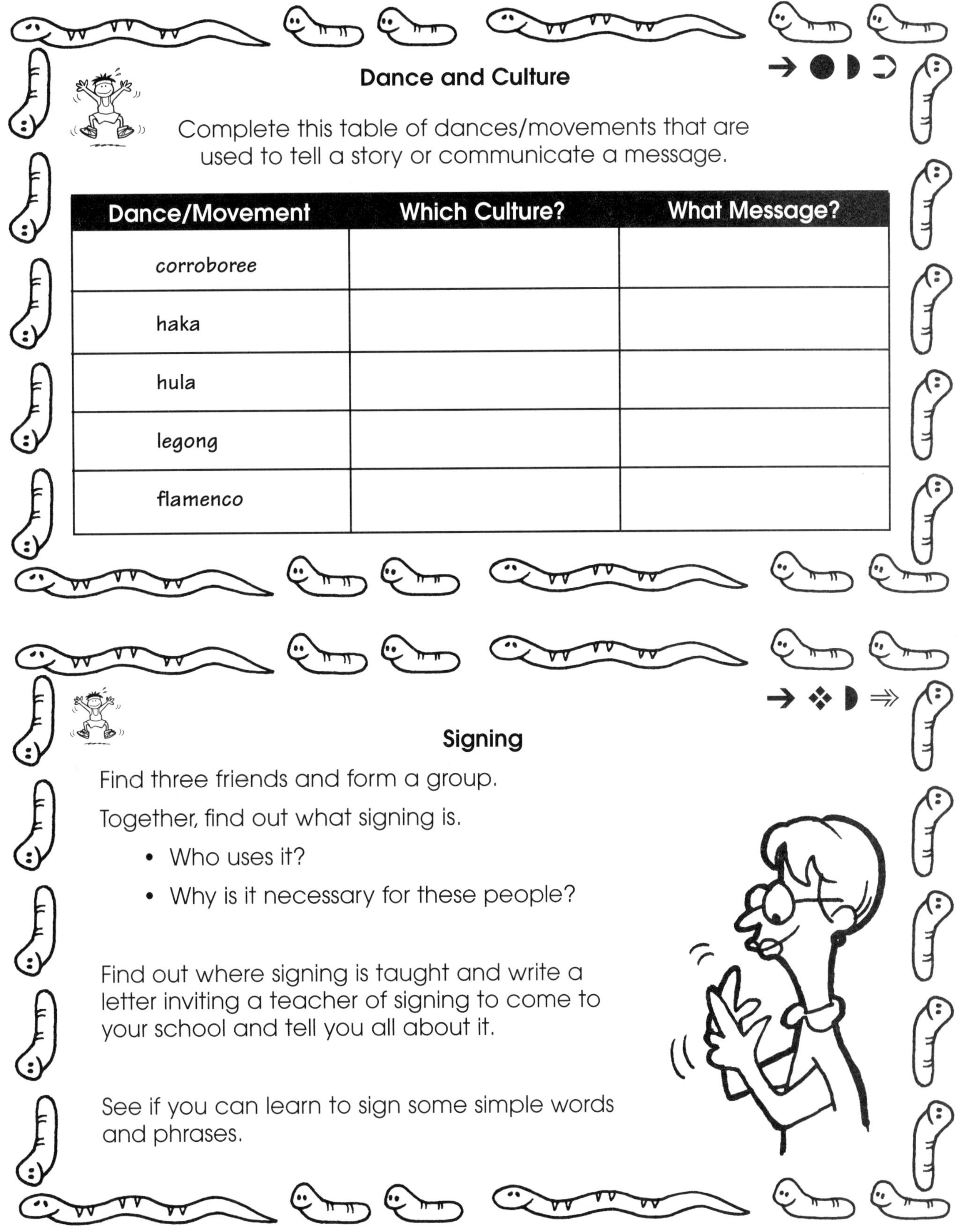

Dance and Culture

Complete this table of dances/movements that are used to tell a story or communicate a message.

Dance/Movement	Which Culture?	What Message?
corroboree		
haka		
hula		
legong		
flamenco		

Signing

Find three friends and form a group.

Together, find out what signing is.

- Who uses it?
- Why is it necessary for these people?

Find out where signing is taught and write a letter inviting a teacher of signing to come to your school and tell you all about it.

See if you can learn to sign some simple words and phrases.

Name:

Management Strategies:

Louis Braille

1. Who was Louis Braille?

Write a short paragraph about Louis Braille and his work.

How important do you think Louis Braille's achievements have been for people who are visually impaired?

2. Write your name in Braille.

Use dots in the space below. If you push through the dots from behind with a pin you will be able to feel the raised paper.

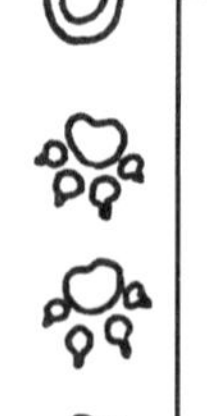

 © Teacher Created Materials, Inc.

Name:

Test Your Miming Ability

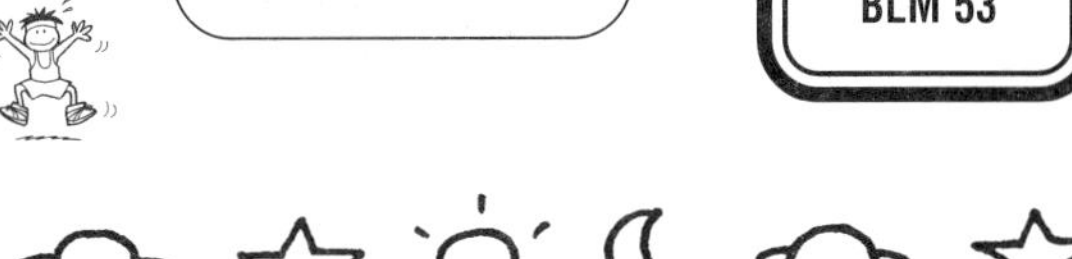

1. **Find a partner.**

   Decide who will be the "subject" and who will be the "helper." The subject wears earplugs and remains silent but active throughout recess. The helper makes sure that any accidents are avoided.

2. **What do you think will be the most difficult part of the experiment?**

   Write your ideas below:

3. **Change roles on the next day.**

   Now write a short summary of your experiment to use for an oral report to the class. (Use the back of the page if necessary.)

GARDNER'S MULTIPLE INTELLIGENCES

TASK CARDS

Activities for Communication

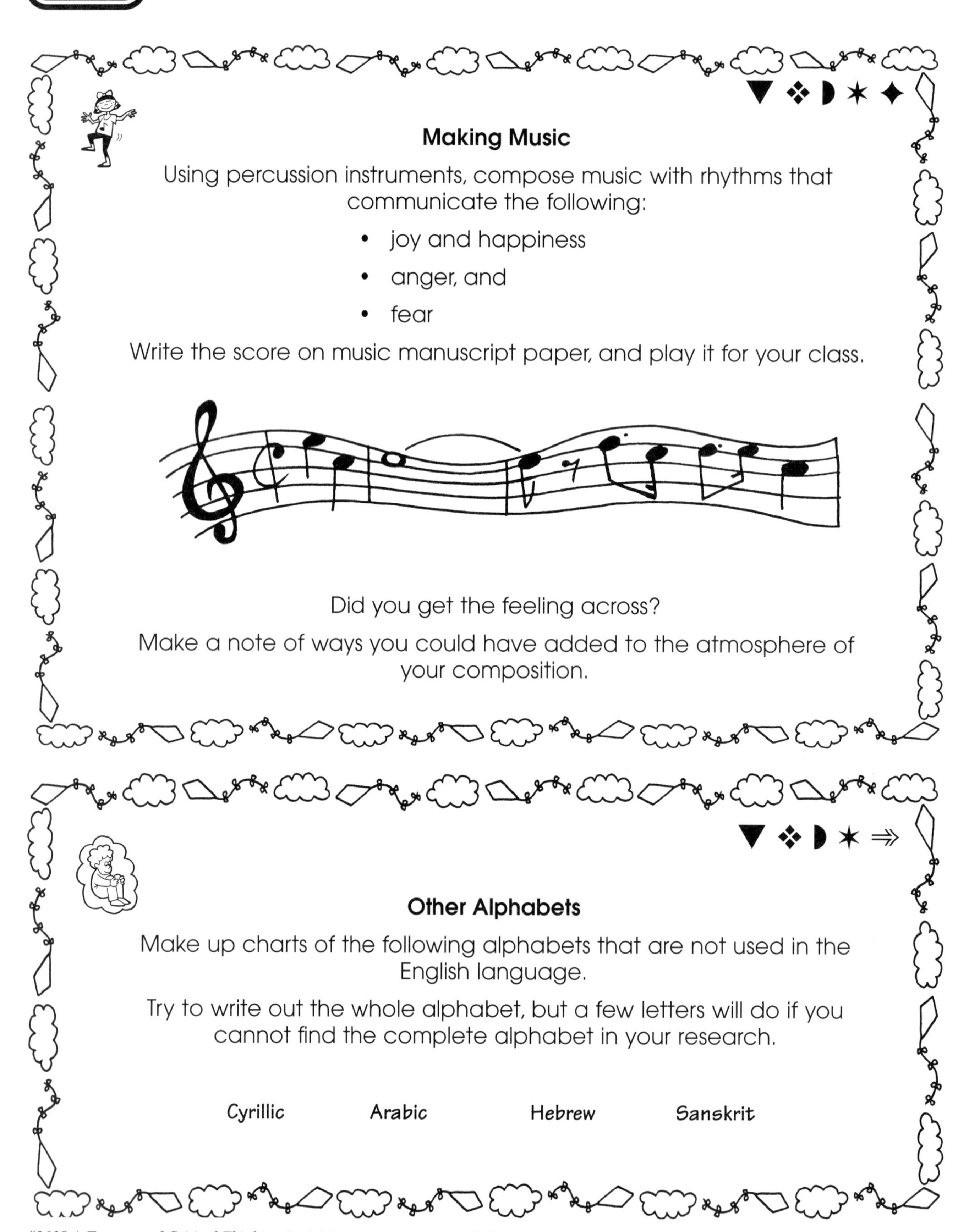

▼ ❖ ◗ ✶ ✦

Making Music

Using percussion instruments, compose music with rhythms that communicate the following:

- joy and happiness
- anger, and
- fear

Write the score on music manuscript paper, and play it for your class.

Did you get the feeling across?

Make a note of ways you could have added to the atmosphere of your composition.

▼ ❖ ◗ ✶ ⇛

Other Alphabets

Make up charts of the following alphabets that are not used in the English language.

Try to write out the whole alphabet, but a few letters will do if you cannot find the complete alphabet in your research.

Cyrillic Arabic Hebrew Sanskrit

© Teacher Created Materials, Inc.

Name:

Making Instruments

1. **Flute**

   Make a primitive "flute" like a small recorder—one that might have been made by people 5,000 years ago.

   Use any material you think could give a successful result.

   Plan your instrument here:

2. **Drum**

   Now make an instrument that could be used as a drum. Use any material that will give a good sound.

   Plan your instrument here:

Prepare a short talk on how you made these instruments, the tools you used, and the time it took. Present your talk to the class after you have demonstrated your instruments.

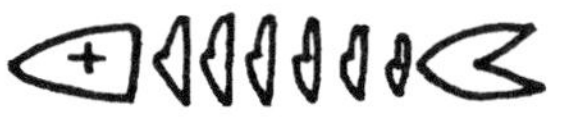

GARDNER'S MULTIPLE INTELLIGENCES

BLM 55

Name:

Communication Types

Fill in the table below.

In column 2, check if **you** use the method listed.

In columns 3 and 4, write down who **would** or **would not** have used the method listed.

Give as many answers as you can.

1. Method	2. You	3. Would use	4. Would not use
Speech			
Letters			
Telephone			
Radio			
Television			
Art			
Music			
Books/Stories			
Computer			
Drums			
Smoke			
Dance			
Telegraph			
Semaphore			

 © Teacher Created Materials, Inc.

Activities for Communication

▼ → ● ❖

Cuneiform and Hieroglyphs

Find the information to complete this table:

Method	Who used it?	Where?	When?	What was it?
Cuneiform				
Hieroglyphs				

● ❖ ■ ✶ ⊃

Save the Environment Scrapbook

Make a note of where you will find articles about the environment:

____

____

____

Collect newspaper clippings and magazine articles about projects that are intended to improve the environment.

Concentrate on those involving communication networks.

Develop a class **Save the Environment Scrapbook.**

GARDNER'S MULTIPLE INTELLIGENCES

BLM 56

Name:

Great Inventors

Management Strategies:

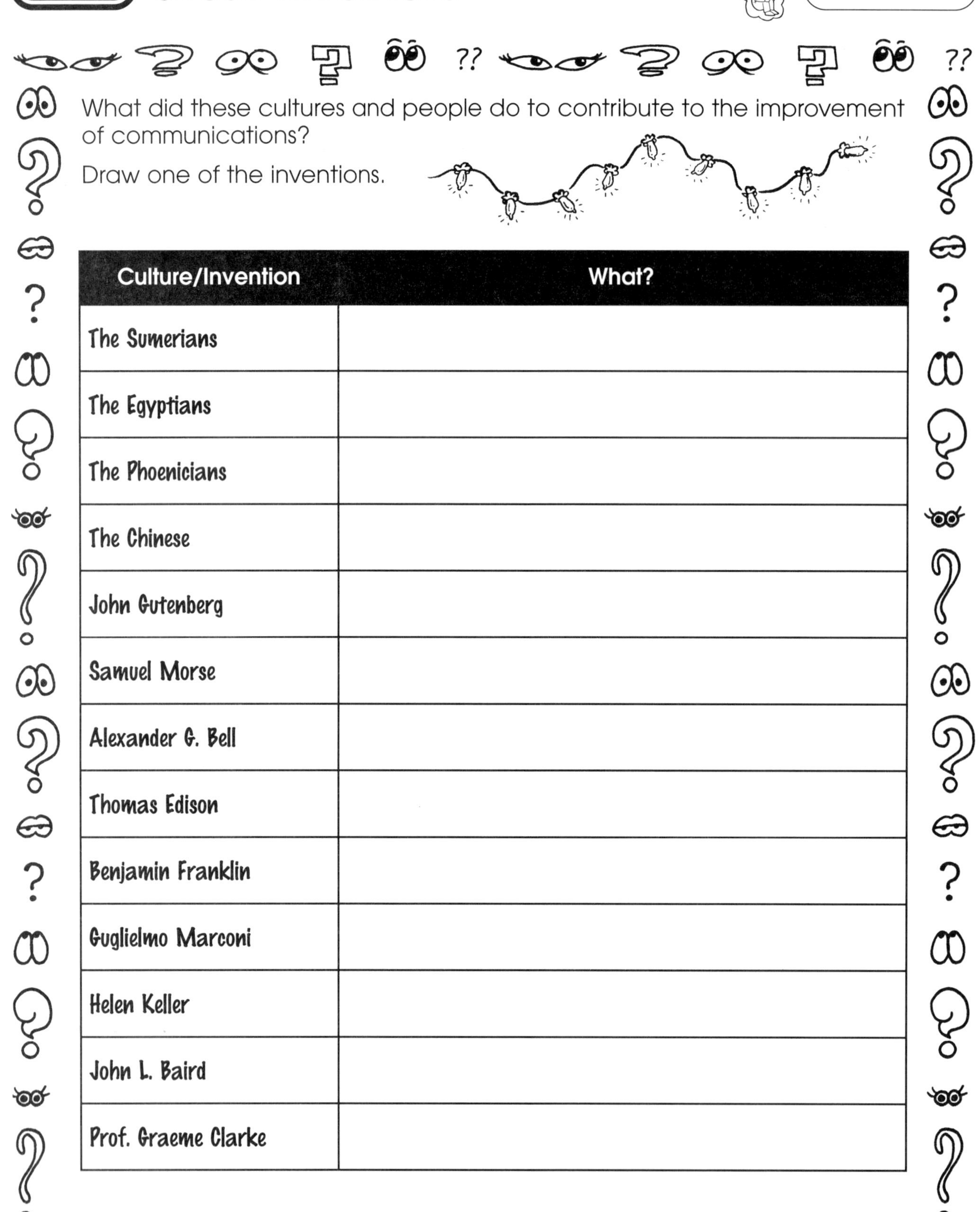

What did these cultures and people do to contribute to the improvement of communications?

Draw one of the inventions.

Culture/Invention	What?
The Sumerians	
The Egyptians	
The Phoenicians	
The Chinese	
John Gutenberg	
Samuel Morse	
Alexander G. Bell	
Thomas Edison	
Benjamin Franklin	
Guglielmo Marconi	
Helen Keller	
John L. Baird	
Prof. Graeme Clarke	

 © Teacher Created Materials, Inc.

Name:

Environment Watch

1. List all the types of environmental damage that can be done in the name of better communication networks. We have started the list for you:

   Television aerials, removal of trees and vegetation, ____________________

   ____

   ____

   ____

2. Take photographs or draw pictures of these types of damage.

   Create a collage poster using these pictures and display it in the school corridor for all to see.

   Plan your poster here.

3. Invite suggestions from classmates, teachers, and parents on ways to repair the damage and avoid further damage.

GARDNER'S MULTIPLE INTELLIGENCES

BLM 58

Name:

Habitat Watch

1. List how the spread of the communication networks affects native animals. We have started the list for you.

Bats get electrocuted on the power lines, ______________________

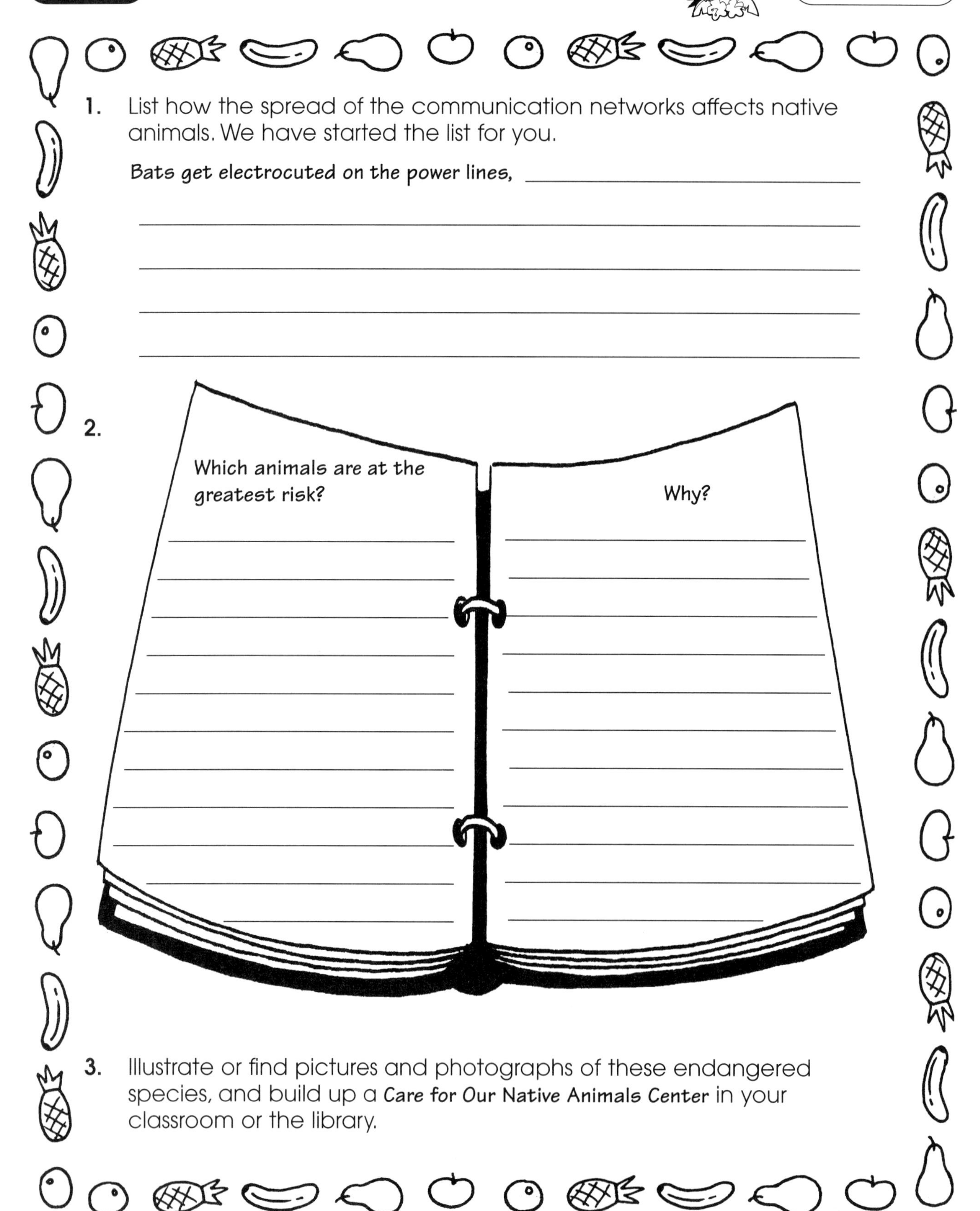

3. Illustrate or find pictures and photographs of these endangered species, and build up a **Care for Our Native Animals Center** in your classroom or the library.

 © Teacher Created Materials, Inc.

Make Your Own Task Cards

Critical Thinking

ACTIVITY BOOK

NOTES

Notes

 © Teacher Created Materials, Inc.